Upon a Sleepless Isle

Andrew Fidel Fernando is a Colombo-based writer and satirist, working mainly for ESPNcricinfo. He travels, eats, cooks, scuba dives, regularly bungles all of the above, and relishes collecting stories that grapple with history and lay bare the soul of a place, particularly his native Sri Lanka. This book, a labour of love, is his first.

Praise for *Upon a Sleepless Isle*

'For its assured story-telling, keen observation, dry humour and sensitive navigation of complex and difficult truths; its effortless intertwining of fact and fable, history and anecdote in a rich tapestry of characters; for its incisive yet empathetic exploration of the ethos of a multicultural people grappling with its post-war realities, religious tensions and deep ethnic binds; a literary work that is both engaging and judicious in its descriptive writing of place, its tracing of the cartographies of memory and landscape, combining and creating a multitude of narrative pathways through a rich terrain of material. For its presentation of a nuanced and insightful reflection of the cultural, political and historical context of a country through the medium of a contemporary traveller's tale, the Gratiaen Prize 2019 is awarded to *Upon A Sleepless Isle* by Andrew Fidel Fernando'
Gratiaen Prize Citation

'A hilarious, nuanced and elegant work that grapples with Sri Lanka's complexities, and celebrates its beauty'
Shehan Karunatilaka, author of the Booker Prize-winning *The Seven Moons of Maali Almeida*

'Utterly engaging, wickedly funny, and quite heroic'
Business Standard

'Unpredictable, hilarious, and informative'
Daily Mirror

'Full of vivid descriptions … engaging and entertaining'
Hindustan Times

'A sincere and original work by an intelligent observer with a keen sense of place'
Mint Lounge

'A heartfelt, compelling read'
Outlook Traveller

'A compelling capture of Sri Lanka's irrepressible character and a textured patina of life, love and loss'
Sunday Island

'A book modern Sri Lanka needed'
The Critic

Upon a Sleepless Isle

ANDREW FIDEL FERNANDO

PICADOR INDIA

First published 2019 by Picador India
First published in paperback 2023 by Picador India
an imprint of Pan Macmillan Publishing India Private Limited
707 Kailash Building
26 K. G. Marg, New Delhi 110001
www.panmacmillan.co.in

Pan Macmillan, The Smithson, 6 Briset Street, London EC1M 5NR
Associated companies throughout the world
www.panmacmillan.com

ISBN 978-93-95624-45-9

Map and illustrations by Ruwangi Amarasinghe
(Fold Media Collective Pvt. Ltd.)

4

Typeset by R. Ajith Kumar, New Delhi
Printed and bound in India at Repro India Ltd., Mumbai

FSC www.fsc.org
MIX
Paper from responsible sources
FSC® C047271

To Fidelia and Sarath

Contents

Nainativu
Jaffna
Kilinochchi
Mannar
Madhu
Trincomalee
Anuradhapura
Minneriya
Pollonnaruwa
Batticaloa
Kaudumunna
Kandy
Negombo
Paranagama
Adams Peak
Arugam Bay
Colombo
Kumana
Sinharaja
Yala
Hambantota
Weligama
Galle

ONE

Little Lords of a Little Street

The smiles in Sri Lanka are as wide as the horizon, visitors say. The nation's treasures are as boundless as the ocean, many report. But never let it be forgotten that the ineptitude of the government is as vast and as awesome as the heavens, as well. So, before I have set foot on a golden curve of sand, or slapped eyes on a verdant spread of paddies, I was in a government office, sat on a puke-green chair, staring at stained beige walls. It was perhaps the ideal place to start any Sri Lankan journey, because brushes with government have a way of filling you with confidence. No matter what mishaps befall your travels, nothing could be worse than what you have endured.

This humid morning was my second attempt at wangling a national identity card out of the local representatives in my hometown of Dehiwala. My first application, handed over about two weeks after I returned to reside in Sri Lanka in 2012, had vanished without a trace somewhere in the nation's bureaucratic maze. That was at least what I was told, though, frankly, I had my doubts. It was much more likely that on the other side of the island, a half-blind old woman had been charged with fraud for mistakenly receiving, then inadvertently presenting, my identity card to officials there. For Sri Lanka's governance is not just consistently inefficient, it is reliably counterproductive. During a long-overdue council upgrade of the drains of south Dehiwala, engineers knocked down a neighbour's kitchen wall, refused him damages, then abandoned the project entirely. Every time monsoon rains fall, neighbourhood drains continue to become a mosquito-breeding fantasyland.

Inside the small office now, I was afforded glimpses at the misshapen parts that comprised the spluttering machinery. From a wooden desk towards the centre of the room, yellowing sheaves of official documents threatened to cascade to the chipped, brushed-cement floor. Papers were stacked like this in government offices all over the country. I suspect this was because if the files fell, Sri Lankan bureaucrats could refuse to acknowledge their existence. Those documents became the cleaners' problem. Sometimes the papers were sold on to roadside food vendors, who made packets out of them. I had once eaten peanuts out of a birth certificate. In a corner of this government room, a Honda Pleasure – presumably belonging to one of the staff – was perfectly positioned to obstruct access to the steel cabinet behind it. Next to the parked scooter, a doorway was guarded by a vacant desk.

Near the entrance, a pudgy man with a faraway grin sat back in his rattan-weave chair. Next to him a woman in a black-and-silver sari, who sat at the adjacent desk, alternated between reading papers and staring at a spot on the wall. These two were quintessential bureaucrats, specializing in distant looks and unabashed idleness. So many government departments seemed to be staffed by people who considered arriving at work their primary task for the day.

Even if you had the financial means to inspire a government worker out of apathy, incompetence would form a second barrier. Many Sri Lankan bureaucrats are unable to handle more than one piece of information at a time, forget more than one task. And they are incapable of acting with speed. Dressed in her gorgeous sari, the woman occasionally rose to fetch files from a wooden drawer in the opposite corner of the room, but she might have lost a foot race to a millipede. The man by the entrance had one form to stamp but spent an enterprising five minutes looking for the inkpad, which he eventually discovered under a file about a foot from his face. In a way it is a good thing these people were born in modern-day Sri Lanka, for what other job in human history would have tolerated them?

It is as if Sri Lanka's bureaucrats followed an alternate course of evolution. Having come to life in a primordial soup of bribes, backhanders, and political favours, these folks have, over billions of years, become perfectly adapted to raising the blood pressure of their patrons.

Just about the only thing bureaucrats enjoy more than idleness, however, is making the public feel small. Of this everyone in the office was soon reminded. When a middle-aged lady ahead of me in the queue requested the form that would permit her to fell a dying jackfruit tree in her garden, it was with the sharp, condescending tone so natural to people in her profession that the bureaucrat responded.

'Tell me exactly where this tree you are talking about is located,' she snapped.

'It's just off Hill Street, about 300 metres from here.'

'Are you sure that neighbourhood comes under the purview of this office?'

'Yes, miss, it's about 300 metres from here.'

You could tell by her composure that the lady had been in skirmishes with government officers before. Losing your temper with a public servant was among the greatest follies of Sri Lankan life. Raise your voice in a government office and you risked being cast into clerical purgatory, your documents and applications forever doomed to be flung atop swaying towers of peanut-packets-to-be.

'That may be, but an environmental officer has to sign off on the removal of protected trees before you can fill out the form.'

The woman had come prepared. 'Yes, someone had had a look and he gave me this,' she said, handing over a slip of paper. This was glanced over with suspicion. 'But he said I needed to fill out another form.'

'Do you have any photographs of this tree?'

'No, but you could come and look at the tree yourself if you'd like. It's about 300 metres from here.'

Only now, faced with the prospect of having to do some work, did the bureaucrat come clean. 'We actually don't have any of the jackfruit tree forms left. They haven't been delivered to us for two months.'

Somehow, the rest of us in the office knew that this was always going to be the outcome of this exchange. Perhaps in the back of her mind, the lady did too. She had one final question: 'Is there any chance you know when the forms will next be in?'

The bureaucrat looked down at her papers and uttered the only sentence you are required to know to gain employment in the Sri Lankan government: 'Check again next week.'

Eventually it was my turn. The Grama Niladhari (village official), under whose auspices the clotted capillaries of government meet the public, was a short man, who looked about forty-five. His wispy hair stood on end and trembled towards the heavens every time the table fan blew in his direction. Barely two minutes had passed since I hurdled that vacant desk to enter his office than he had dispatched me to obtain two more documents from a local Justice of the Peace (JP). When I asked him where the closest JP might be found, the Grama Niladhari waved his right hand through the air, gesturing roughly in the direction of the rest of the universe.

Resolved to hand over my application the same morning, I quickly located a JP, but to no avail. His daughter had dropped his official seal a week ago. The repair shop had been infernally slow in returning it.

In the end I was forced to prevail on the kindness of the nearby Buddhist temple, whose head monk had the authority to certify the documents I required. 'We should get these stamped straight away,' he said, throwing his saffron robe over his shoulder to retrieve his stationery from the other room.

'You know, the Grama Niladhari goes at 11:30 for lunch and the fellow doesn't come back afterwards.'

His urgency was for nothing. I had hoped, perhaps foolishly, to take advantage of the express service through which, theoretically, you could receive your card within the same day. It was in fact to gain a pre-clearance for that process that I had even come to the Grama Niladhari. But soon as I handed in my application, I was told the whole thing would take around three weeks, due to my not having applied before the age of twenty. There was, I was assured, no way around the delay. This was something of a problem since I had planned to set out on my travels in a few days.

I decided to do without it. I didn't exactly need the card, I supposed. I still had the passport that had served as my identification document in the past four years. Only, I worried about the state it was in. Following many rounds of rough and tumble in jeans pockets and backpacks, my passport had begun to exhibit the signs of a hard life. Most pages were frayed or crumpled, and the cover was denuding itself of its brown-red gloss to reveal powdery cardboard beneath. Though some years remained before its official expiry, to look at the passport now, it was pleading to be euthanized. There were also portions of the island in which – the most part of a decade following the end of a long civil war – a national identity card would be the least suspicious documentation to carry. But, vanquished thus by the bureaucracy, I returned home to prepare for the trip.

Dehiwala had been a sleepy Colombo suburb in my childhood. I remember when my friends and I ruled our little street. We rode bicycles on the road in the morning, then sent up kites in the afternoon when the wind blew strong off the sea. Street cricket matches went uninterrupted by traffic for hours, and even when cars did come along, we'd carry on. This made a lot of motorists angry. When a series of agitated honks failed to displace us, they would charge out of their vehicles, fists clenched, globs of saliva and savage threats filling the air. Only when we had moved a driver to the edge of insanity did we finally shuffle off and let the vehicle pass. We would then reclaim our pitch and resume play until a murderous vortex was made of the next driver. The only people who could immediately bring a match to an end were our mothers, who at dusk every day would yank us home by our ears.

Back when Dehiwala streets were sleepy, and the little lords ruled.

But in the years that I had been abroad, the cars had won the war. You could not play cricket on the street anymore. You could barely take a step out of your gate before you were carried off by a torrent of traffic and deposited on a pavement somewhere, two suburbs over. Houses had been built so high, kites could no longer be flown either. Children still tried, in the windy months, but spent most of their time untangling string from overhead telephone lines and scrambling clumsily around on the tiled roofs looking for downed kites. When the rains came, houses for miles around had sprung new leaks.

When I was growing up, we used to have to head halfway into town to buy so much as a newspaper. Now there is a twenty-four-hour pharmacy, a cafe, a large bookshop, a supermarket, a vehicle dealer, and two hair salons all within 600 metres of my parents' home. I could leave the house on foot and be back within the hour with a latte, a fauxhawk and a hybrid car – all spectacles that would have brought neighbours out onto their verandahs in years gone by.

The only thing in Dehiwala that hasn't changed is the corner shop across the road from the house. It is a tiny hole-in-the-wall place that has been out of virtually anything you need to buy for about three decades. There is never any bread in this shop, no flour, no rice, no soap, no cellphone credit. But whenever you visit, the shopkeeper – a squat lady with graying hair and a nasal voice – will unfailingly produce an improbable explanation as to why stock is running so low. 'Oh what a shame you didn't come looking for toothpaste just a little earlier,' she might say. 'We had plenty this morning. This whole shelf was full of toothpaste. But then a man from a few roads down came and bought it all, just like that. Taking a group on a trip, apparently. I didn't want to sell so much at once, you know, because I knew other people needed it, but he insisted. What could I do?' The purpose of these stories is to suggest that notwithstanding this sudden and particular upsurge in demand, she is running quite the clinical operation.

What the shop genuinely does a booming trade in is gossip. Older ladies from all around make daily visits for the sole purpose of collecting and disseminating scandalous information (though to keep up appearances, they will also ask for half a kilo of sugar and no doubt be told that a large team of horses had only now come by). News spreads at incredible speeds through this network. If an affair has been discovered anywhere within a fifty-kilometre radius, the tantalising details, within hours, will have been served up, digested, and regurgitated at the store.

'How could that dog of a man Manoj do this to our Swarna, who has never had an evil thought in her life?' Most times none of the participants in this conversation have ever laid eyes on the people whose lives are being picked apart, yet a companion will offer: 'Poor thing must be distraught. How is she going to take care of her four children now, with her bad leg and everything? You know I cooked for her every day when she was in hospital after the accident last year. Even then, I could tell Manoj was a snake from the way he was leering at the nurses.' It keeps getting worse until, by the end of the day, the number of Swarna's destitute children has grown to eight and some of them are blind, deaf, or missing a limb.

It's amazing what passes for scandal in my neighbourhood. A young girl wearing a dress that exposes her knees could spark long, speculative conversations on her romantic prospects. If a young man buys a powerful motorbike, he is an ungrateful son, shirking responsibility. Heaven forbid someone gets a tattoo. The whole family would be written off as demon worshippers.

Men are no less given to idle talk. In bars or trishaw stands they speak about who the good-looking actresses are cavorting with, or which minister's son likes to party hardest. Sri Lanka's politics is spectacular fodder, forever enlivened by judicial injunctions, summary firings, trade union turmoil, impromptu travel junkets, roaring nepotism, and institutional drunkenness. Every few months an official is caught entering a public brawl or making a pass at a visiting female dignitary. It is part comedy, part cancer, all embarrassment.

Still, I suppose there must be some competent people in government, because in the years since the war's end, there have been substantial improvements to Sri Lankan life. Dehiwala happens to be just one of many Colombo neighbourhoods that have hurtled towards modernity and cleanliness. Beira Lake – a sixty-five-hectare body of water near the centre of the city – was for so long a cache of dead fish and diseased pelicans but it has been made anew. You can hire swan-shaped pedal boats and genuinely enjoy bobbing about for an hour or two. During the Buddhist festival of Vesak around May, coloured lanterns are strung up over the edge of the lake and hundreds more, in the shape of lotuses or water lilies, are set afloat. Brightly-lit canoes make their way to the island at the centre, which is home to a Buddhist shrine. Families from around Sri Lanka come to frolic in the Beira's ethereal glow. Completing the scene, a dozen *dansal* (alms-giving) stalls on the paved perimeter serve free dinners, coffee, and ice cream.

All over the city, in fact, parks have been transformed into spick-and-span reprieves from the surrounding clutter but these are merely the mellower tokens of progress. Elsewhere, as on the seaside stretch at Galle Face, five-star hotel developments creep upwards and showy new restaurants open their doors every month. When, in June 2015, the Global Destination Cities Index declared Colombo to be the fastest-growing metropolis on the planet, the city really began to buy its own hype. Posh apartment buildings began to burst from the ground in all directions, promising ocean views and opulence. While with one hand, property developers slipped bribes to city regulators, they tickled Colombo's ego with the other, naming the new buildings Regal Residencies, or Pompous Condominiums, or Tax Evasion Towers. This is not a town whose upper crust has ever been short on pretension.

All this growth has seen the city host ever-denser masses of aspirational humanity, of course, and the influx of newcomers has become something of a problem for the municipal council. How to ease pressure on already groaning infrastructure? The council had floated the idea of building a monorail network, before realizing it would cost too much. The government had continued to hike up import taxes on cars, but thanks in part to rising wages, streets continue to be crammed with shiny SUVs. About two years ago, there was a major attempt at making the roads themselves more efficient. The city installed new traffic lights every few hundred metres along the central arteries. These lights had all the trimmings: the separate panels for right and left turning lanes, bright LED lamps that made pedestrian crossings positively sparkle, and instead of ordinary green and red bulbs, there were digital clocks that counted down to the next change of signal. These timers were an excellent addition because so much of the anguish of traffic is in its uncertainty. Now, when gridlocked in Colombo, motorists could see exactly how many seconds they must wait before the light went green and they could continue to remain immobile, because the mass of vehicles ahead was, like them, totally inert. It does not help that many Colombo drivers seem to think the hundreds of kilograms of metal in their control can teleport through other solid objects. In non-peak hours, cars skim merrily across busy main roads, trucks attempt to squeeze through tiny gaps, and motorcycles slalom through packed streets, appearing suddenly into view, then vanishing into a knot of traffic within seconds.

Arguably the city's greatest public menace – the buses – are forever barging into lanes at light-speed, braking and accelerating with abandon, and generally screeching around while their occupants are hurled around the interior like molecules in a large hadron collider. They are also armed with deafening horns. One honk on these would adequately alert a large town that a meteor was about to hit. Colombo bus drivers use these billion-decibel eruptions to hurry old ladies across pedestrian crossings.

Trishaws are less dangerous, though that is mainly because of their relative size. Many of their operators are certainly no less insane. Trishaw drivers are fearsome critics of other people's driving, spending whole journeys fuming at vans that veer into their lane, or spraying abuse at motorcyclists trying to overtake on the left. 'Look at this brainless donkey turning right without even turning on his signal,' a driver would seethe, the veins on his forehead in tumult. Meanwhile, his own vehicle has ploughed through a roadside mango stall.

I do love this city. This was something of a surprise. When I returned home as an adult, I had hoped, eventually, to find my way to Kandy, where I would have a garden hammock to sling myself in, and a view of a lush hillside to breathe in every morning. Yet Colombo's chaos grew on me. Now, if I am away too long, I find myself hankering for the noise, the smell of the sea, and the bus rides where everyone aboard sports expanding sweat circles beneath the arm.

But, for this returning Sri Lankan, coming to grips with the island's biggest city was not nearly enough. I had been a child of the wartime years, when bombs exploding within earshot of our home had inspired a deep-seated dread of travel within my parents. Even if we did venture a brief journey, half-a-dozen military checkpoints seemed to stand between the front door and the gate. So much as a forgotten handbag could empty carriages and hold trains up for hours, while bomb squads checked for explosives. The kind of long, rambling out-of-town adventures I had dreamt of as a child were largely out of the question. The best I could do, back then, was gaze longingly at the map and merely imagine the salt flats of the northwest, the palmyrah groves of the northern peninsula, and the leopards in the untamed southeast.

Since coming home again, I had visited some of the better-known Sri Lankan destinations, but these trips were often brief and unsatisfying – never more than a few days in length and generally only undertaken for the purposes of my work as a cricket writer. Also, as if to rub salt into this wound, wealthy foreigners began to waltz on to the island, posting pictures from national parks I had craved to visit for decades and towns that had intrigued me since my childhood. In the post-war years, the world had made Sri Lanka a hip all-round destination thanks to its abundance of beaches, mountains, delicious food, history, and – if some travel magazines were to be believed – Sri Lankans so friendly you could kick them in their Sri Lankan gonads and still fail to wipe the smiles off their Sri Lankan faces.

On the verge of turning twenty-eight now, I no longer wished to be a stranger to the delights of my own land. Upon my childhood wonderments, new questions had been layered. How did northern towns fare while the nation attempted peace? Did the southern belt thrive now that tourism had boomed for half-a-decade? Was post-war prosperity being shared by the tea-bearing central mountains? There was wildlife to encounter and hilltops to scale, panting, only for the view to take what was left of my breath away. There were freshly rebuilt train tracks to ply and bright new roads to hurtle along in *baila*-blasting provincial buses. I dreamed of waking up and deciding where next to go on a whim, without ever bringing sandbagged military barricades into the reckoning – a freedom Sri Lankans had not enjoyed for three decades.

I did have to convince my wife Erena, a New Zealander who had taken swiftly to Sri Lankan life in our four years here, to let me hit the road for an indefinite stretch. So supernaturally kind and understanding is she that this did not prove much of a challenge. Her only request was that she joined me for the occasional weekend, as her work schedule allowed.

So, just after dawn on a September morning, before the heat and the commuting masses had begun their war on the city, I slipped out the front gate of my childhood home and found myself in a trishaw headed north. I could hear the ocean. It was roaring.

TWO

A Spray of Watery Indents

'If the British had never come to Ceylon, we still wouldn't be having any railroads,' my Tamil grandmother used to say. She was a small, tenacious woman who in the 60s and 70s raised three children by herself on a measly schoolteacher's salary. My grandmother firmly believed that she had been equipped for this triumph by the pre-independence education she received at a British-run school. Accordingly, her loyalties were somewhat muddled. The history she had been weaned on was warped.

For many in her generation, the rail network had become a sort of hallmark of British superiority: the blade at the end of the spear they threw at the government. 'This bloody country has only gone downhill since the British left,' was another commonly heard senior complaint, usually followed by, 'Sri Lanka has had no proper order for decades,' and then an abrupt daytime nap during which the soup they had been eating was incrementally spilt upon themselves.

Yet, since the island ceased to be an outpost of Empire, it has made loping advances by most metrics. Immunizations are virtually universal. A literacy rate north of ninety-two is the envy of the region. Under the public housing scheme many of the poorest Sri Lankans have shelter. And additionally, no one grows those poofy Victorian beards that flies can lay eggs in or makes daily assaults on their own innards with corsets.

All this is a circuitous way to suggest my grandmother's prospectus on the railroads could do with an update. Sri Lanka has by no means covered itself in glory since 1948, the government having oppressed a minority badly enough over several decades to spark a civil war. Nevertheless, a more historically sensible synopsis of the old days might be: The British racially subjugated an entire people for 130 years, massacred thousands, and maliciously sowed ethnic discord, but at least were not so lacking in human decency at the time of their reluctant departure as to dismantle the infrastructure they had used to so extravagantly plunder the country's resources.

So as I arrived in Colombo's Fort Station and made my way towards a northeast-bound train, how could I help but be overcome with pride at the distance Sri Lanka had come? How thrilled I was not to be travelling in one of those filthy, loud, diesel-powered monstrosities from the 1930s! Instead, I was boarding a filthy, loud, diesel-powered monstrosity from the 1980s. This train even had rotating ceiling fans and overhead lights all through the carriages. Yes, so what if most fans were defunct and festooned with rust? Who cares if the lights were only powerful enough to attract insects? This, friends, was progress.

I clambered aboard an empty carriage, found a seat to my liking, and wrestled the window open. The sounds of Fort Station washed through the car. The place is a people watcher's paradise in the early morning. School children in pristine whites poured from incoming trains: the boys largely half-asleep and lumbering into solid objects, girls stereotypically peppy, and already organized into giggly groups. Office workers in shirt-and-tie or smart saris moved with keener purpose, positively fleeing from their trains to avoid being lodged at the back of a bottleneck at the station exit.

People travel from as far as Kandy to work in Colombo. It is not uncommon to endure a daily round trip of five hours. Over months and years, commuters develop specific commuting habits and make commuting friends for whom they save seats and play cards with. Couples I know have even fallen in love on long rides to work. In many trains there is a pair flirting coyly with each other while the rest of the cabin pretends not to be straining to hear their every word. This all seems very sweet, only, for every man that works up the courage to make his move on a lady, there are a hundred men that never overcome the creepy staring phase.

While the PA system reeled off announcements in melancholy monotone, vendors hawking food and drink in pleading squawks cut through the ambient burble. I had almost fallen asleep when a man with a tall, pink flask tore through my carriage, yawping. For forty rupees, I received a paper cup of coffee loaded with enough sugar to sweeten a swimming pool. The drink's perking effects were soon undone by my next purchase: *parippu vadai*, the lightly-spiced disks of fried lentil that are crunchy on the outside, crumbly at the centre, and inarguably one of the greatest travelling snacks. A bagful of these in the belly, I began to nod off again. At some point, we must have pulled out of the station. When consciousness eventually returned, the grubby concrete of the city had dissolved; instead, palms, golden paddies, and wetlands were sweeping by.

Inside, I had gained about a dozen carriage-mates: two families and a few young couples. Minutes later, an elderly gentleman limped down the aisle, begging. His was not a bad haul; in this carriage alone, he collected enough for a fairly nutritious meal. Generosity in Sri Lanka was a curious thing. At the Dehiwala corner shop, I'd heard tales of a beggar woman who removed haggard daytime wigs and bounced around in finery on the weekends and of men who had sawed their own arms off in the eighties and now lived in a three-storey home. The purpose here was to justify tightfistedness. Yet when many come face-to-face with hardship, a charitable instinct kicks in. In 2015, Sri Lanka was placed eighth on a World Giving Index. I've seen Colombo beggars counting wads of small notes in the open. Passersby continue to press money into their hands.

Teaks and jackfruit trees began to appear as the train juddered inland on a northeastern heading, as the loamy soil of the western province gave way to harder, drier earth. Clattering by were little whitewashed houses with asbestos roofing; T-shirts, dresses, and jeans hanging from lines that sprang between fruit trees in backyards. Every fifteen minutes or so a town took unruly shape: its buses trumpeting, its CD stores booming with baila, and its vegetable sellers armed with dishcloths to fight their losing war against the flies. Only the railway crossings brought the streets to a temporary truce, a medley of vehicles watching impatiently from behind each set of lowered barricades. The moment the trailing carriage was clear, their scrum was rejoined.

It was only in the last ninety minutes of my journey that civilization really loosened its grip. We had passed coconut and rubber plantations that had gone uninterrupted for acres but the little farmland that remained to view produced hardier crops: onion, chillies, finger millet. A little after the town of Maho, the tracks began splitting thick jungle. Mahoganies, satinwoods, and palu trees stood out, but the undergrowth had a parched look – this being the final month of Sri Lanka's long, dry season. There was a light spray from the heavens near Kalawewa. It was five minutes to midday when I disembarked at the small town of Habarana.

Had I travelled by car, I might not have arrived until at least two hours later. There are only 190 kilometres of road between Colombo and Habarana, which should make for a four-hour journey. Only, much of that route was now beset by roadworks. Construction has been ongoing for so many years on the forested stretch between Kurunegala and Dambulla that the only reasonable use of time will be if Sri Lanka's transport authority unveils a wormhole between the two cities. Instead, what the public will get is a standard dual carriageway. So many new vehicles will have taken to the roads during the years of its construction, there will be no discernible change in traffic.

The station at Habarana was little more than a large, well-kept shelter with a high, sloping roof, two wooden benches painted green, and a cluttered ticket office. Near the exit at the far end of the station's only platform, a dark, slim man in a red polo shirt stood twirling keys in his right hand. The moment I was within earshot, he offered me a ride in his trishaw.

He was in the mood to chat as he took me to a guesthouse and I soon learned why. A salvo of his questions began with: 'Where are you coming from?' Then: 'Did you come alone?' And: 'What do you do?' Which was just to warm me up for: 'So what are you doing here?' I told him I was looking to safari at the nearby Minneriya National Park. This is just what he wanted to hear. 'My brother and I run a safari jeep,' he said. When he turned to face me, a grin now cleaved his face in two. 'Why don't we go in the afternoon?' Having no better plan of action, I agreed to have them pick me up at 2:30. 'Anyway, there's no point going before then, no? The elephants don't come out in this heat.'

'It is possible that in no other part of the world are there to be found within the same space, the remains of so many works for irrigation, which are at the same time of such great antiquity and of such vast magnitude as in Ceylon.'

So wrote a British government agent by the name of J. Bailey in 1859, of the most distinctive accomplishment of

Sri Lanka's ancient kingdom: its awe-inspiring plexus of man-made reservoirs, streams, bunds, and channels. Faced with an increasing demand for rice and the vagaries of a climate that is intolerably dry for eight months and unbearably wet for four, almost every ancient and medieval ruler of note took on a big irrigation project. A close look at a map of the north central province reveals a landscape that appears to have had a giant shotgun fired at it from space, the spray of pellets leaving watery indents of various shapes and sizes. Among the first renovations on the land was Minneriya Lake. Built during the reign of King Mahasen in the third century, the lake covered nineteen square kilometres and irrigated an expanse perhaps ten times that size. It is vital now, just as it was when it was first built, with agriculture comprising the guts of the local economy.

What Mahasen may not have envisioned is the profound impact the lake has had on the flora and fauna of the region, over 1,700 years. Where once lay semi-arid scrubland now stands seventy square kilometres of dense forest, colonized by all manner of tropical species. There are the immense bulging canopies of banyan and bodhi trees from which leer tittering troupes of langurs and macaques. Below them peacocks, wild boar, mongooses, and jungle fowl prosper amid flowering Indian lilacs, crown flower shrubs and ponds spangled with water lilies.

The most unique vegetation is the green bamboo, which grows here in large and curious bundles. Several hundred clump together in an area the rough circumference of the centre circle of a football pitch. They slant upwards tightly around each other until, at about four metres high, the clump cinches like the waist of a woman's dress. The stems continue upwards for seven or eight further metres and fan out at the top, the tallest among them describing a gentle downward curve.

The bamboo groves were among the first attractions we encountered upon entering Minneriya National Park, just before 3 pm. The trishaw driver, Dhammika, sat in the back of the open-top jeep with me while his brother Sajith drove us. 'Fellows in town are always asking me to cut down a few of these when we come,' Dhammika said jerking in his seat as the jeep bounced along the dirt road. 'If you can put your aerial on top, the pretty actresses on TV become even prettier.' He laughed to himself. 'But then I'd also never be allowed in the park again.'

We rattled on past the bamboos, forded a narrow stream and spooked a few spotted deer as Dhammika chattered cheerfully on. Within half an hour, I had learned of his many travails: his father had turned to alcohol for the past five years and had not earned a living for even longer. His mother had taken odd jobs around the village until, two weeks ago, she was bitten by a viper while harvesting onions. She had only begun to walk again the previous day. He had a sister, too, who was in her final year at a local high school. And a wife who was expecting their first child. His mother-in-law had just arrived in town recently, to coach the couple through the final months of the pregnancy.

He was optimistic. If tourism continued to boom, he thought, he and his brother would pay off the loan on the jeep in three years. 'We're getting all kinds these days: English, Germans, Chinese, Japanese, Indians, Arabs, Russians. The only thing is, the tourists we get now are different from the ones we had years ago, before the war ended. Those days a foreigner would stop and talk and give a child a lollipop or something. Now they come in huge numbers. They just want to see the attractions and go.'

Sajith pounded the brakes when he spotted a monitor lizard, almost by force of habit, but took off again quickly when he saw I was unenthused. Reptiles are often a thrill for foreigners. For Sri Lankans – even those from the cities – they are humdrum, a feature of daily life. Monitors had been frequent visitors to my parents' back garden in Dehiwala and, in our younger years, my sisters and I used to flee when we spotted them below our belli tree. Recently, a salt-water crocodile had been seen on Dehiwala beach. Not long before that, a gang of babblers attacked and killed what looked to me like a young hump-nosed viper, just outside our back door.

Animals in general are almost as prolific in urban Sri Lanka as they are in the jungle. Stray dogs are the most obvious example. Explanations as to why Sri Lanka has so many strays centre around the two main religions – Buddhism and Hinduism – that both advocate care for living things. It is not uncommon for people to leave food out for the strays in their neighbourhood, for example. In 2006, a presidential order banned the extermination of stray dogs as a means of population control.

Whatever the cause, what is beyond doubt is that Sri Lanka is effectively a sixteen-million-acre sex party for small animals. Everywhere you look in the country, they are going at it. Dogs are seen mating on virtually every street corner and backyard and, on many occasions, in the background of television field news reports. Cat sex is no less prevalent, though thankfully, a little less public. The worst offenders of all are household geckos. They are everywhere you look in a Sri Lankan house, chasing each other up walls, wriggling around furniture, and leaving white-tipped mini-droppings on window ledges. Almost every week there seem to be fresh young. People seem generally happy to have geckos around, believing they help keep unwelcome insects at bay, yet there's no shortage of flies and mosquitoes anywhere. More than likely, the geckos are too tired from all the action to do anything about the insects.

A few minutes after we left the monitor lizard behind, we came upon what I had really travelled to see. I glimpsed a hind leg through the trees at first, then a bulging grey body, then a tip of a trunk, and then all of a sudden, as the jungle gave way to wide-open expanse, a herd of about twenty-five elephants hove into view. As we drove on, I realized there was a group of as many elephants beyond this first lot. Then, when the jeep climbed a small mound, yet more – a veritable multitude – became visible, loitering about the lake, about 100 metres away. The numbers were almost overwhelming. By rough count, there must have been at least 150 elephants in our line of sight.

This, in all its glory, was The Gathering of Minneriya, where, in the height of the dry season, about 500 elephants converge on the lake from as far as Trincomalee. It is the greatest recurring assembly of elephants on the planet and, arguably, one of the most spellbinding natural sights anywhere. In addition to watering its seasonal throng, Minneriya also feeds its visitors; the lake diminishing to a long finger of deep water, while its rich, expanding banks sprout plumes of grass for the animals to gorge on.

There were so many in such close proximity, it was impossible to tell where one herd ended and another began. There were bull elephants ranging the periphery of large clusters, chasing off unwanted approaches from other males. Occasionally a pair would lock tusks; the larger animal invariably driving back the challenger. Beyond them, scores of females and juveniles fed more peacefully, using the lip on the end of their nozzles to clutch and uproot clumps of grass. They brushed dirt off against a raised foot before lifting it to their angular mouths. Weeks-old baby elephants, playful and clumsy, wove unsteady orbits, while their mothers admonished them with a short harrumph if ever they strayed. By the lake, some elephants sprayed water on themselves using their trunks for a spout. Others wallowed in the shallows.

We spent at least two hours driving from group to group, observing each lot for a while, backing off when knots of elephants drew near the jeep, then trailing after others as they moved off into the distance. A young male elephant provided the highlight of the afternoon's entertainment as he made repeated sneaky advances on a female that was being guarded by a larger bull. It began with the young male pretending to be totally uninterested while the big bull eyed him up. You could almost imagine the youngster pretending to whistle idly, with his hands in his pockets, as he faced the other way. As soon as the bull averted his gaze, though, the young male made his move, slinking towards the female like a pantomime burglar approaching a window. The only difference was, this burglar's crowbar was cylindrical, several feet long, and hung near his hind legs. The closer he got to his prize, the larger it grew, looking as it emerged from a wrinkly sheath like a cross between a self-peeling banana and a slowly-extending lightsaber. You could almost hear it go 'whoomph' as it swung from side to side. Just as he positioned himself behind the female, the adult bull caught sight of him again, and came charging with an intimidating trumpet call.

The young male fled, but continued to attempt this surreptitious manoeuvre several times, penis always at the ready. It seemed a foolish pursuit, especially as the adult bull was now wise to his intentions after that first, close call. But I guess that just like with humans, the youngster's brain was operating below capacity, so much of his blood engaged elsewhere. The females, for the most part, ignored the boys' antics, perhaps happy in the knowledge that they only need tolerate males for a few more weeks. When the rains come, and replenished streams and water holes beckon the elephants back into the jungle, males are almost totally cut off from the herds.

Dusk had begun to set in when we made our way out of the park. More elephants had emerged from the trees as the afternoon wore on, and Dhammika guessed we would have seen maybe 200 in total. On some days, he said, you could see as many as 300.

I returned to my guesthouse just before dark, ate a little later at a nearby restaurant, and played the afternoon over in my thoughts as I settled into bed. The Gathering, and the tourists it drew, had been a blessing for men like Dhammika and the town of Habarana in general. I would discover the next day that not everyone in the region was so enthused by the elephants' arrival. In many neighbourhoods, people would be glad never to see one again.

The following morning was unseasonably cool. My guesthouse served up a bland breakfast of bread and jam, which I left half eaten before making my way to the eastbound bus halt near the centre of town. There were about five others there already, mostly women, each one holding aloft an umbrella though there was barely a dark cloud in the sky.

It isn't just rain that sells umbrellas in Sri Lanka. What these people, and many others in the country, fear, of course, is growing a shade or two darker in the sun. This is in keeping with ideals of beauty that stretch back into antiquity, when a fair complexion was a badge of wealth and status. The rich and important avoided labour – and the outdoors.

In the centuries since, colonial influence has lent light skin an extra edge of desirability, and many Sri Lankans will go to extraordinary lengths to achieve it. Skin-whitening soaps do raging business. A cream that promises to turn an ordinary dark-skinned local into someone who could command a battalion in Hitler's master race is probably the most sought-after cosmetic in the land. And many Sri Lankans make sunlight avoidance a feature of their lifestyle. I have a cousin who wears full-sleeved tops and long skirts in the heat, while others prefer to brave the outdoors only around dawn and dusk. Yet more will stay standing in buses and trains over taking a sun-dappled seat. This can become such an obsession that there are probably people who would be happy to be rolled around in a barrel all day if it meant being exposed to fewer rays.

The bus arrived, playing some lively Sri Lankan pop from the 1970s and was soon barreling along itself, around the verdant edge of the national park. I got off at the town of Minneriya and headed for a parked row of trishaws. The first driver I talked to knew exactly the place I was looking for: the spot where, in the last Gathering season, an elephant had killed a man.

There was not much to see anymore. We came to an open space large enough to park about three buses and ringed by tall grass. Next door stood a tiny village shop. The owner of the store, a narrow-limbed, white-haired woman named Asoka, pointed out two untidy rows of trees at the northern end of the sweep and told me that is where the trampling had happened. She had been indoors at the time.

'See, elephants came here all the time before they put that up a few years ago,' she said pointing in the direction of the electric fence that formed the boundary of the jungle, a few hundred metres away. 'Those days they came looking for salt and all, and sometimes broke a wall to get to our food, but very rarely only people were hurt. We knew to stay calm and spoke to them gently. Last year, it wasn't like that. People were over-excited because this was the first elephant in a long time.'

This bull elephant had come up from a village to the northeast called Pasiyawewa. No one knows how it got around the fence; more than likely it came from further afield and had not been inside the electrified park limits in the first place. What is clear is that when it arrived at this field just outside Minneriya town, it was being pursued. A twenty-strong mob of Pasiyawewa locals were giving chase.

Soon enough, people from the Minneriya village were drawn outside by the commotion. The crowd doubled, the elephant was goaded in every direction. 'When elephants are angry, you can tell, no?' said Asoka. 'They will trumpet loudly, and act very aggressive. This fellow was not like that. The people only were agitated. Carrying big sticks and all, they were shouting like anything.'

That the upheaval and eventual tragedy was almost totally man-made could hardly have been clearer. The victim was a forty-six-year-old video journalist, who had only arrived at the scene to cover the incident for a local television outlet; his very presence, artificial. He had also been guilty of following the elephant too closely, to get a tighter shot. When the animal suddenly spun around, the journalist had stumbled, possibly after having become entangled in his video equipment. The trampling, an eyewitness told the news, wasn't really a trampling. The elephant pressed on the man's head with a front leg but had not crushed him completely. When four others later carried him, unconscious, past Asoka's shop, she saw no obvious wounds. It was only later, in the car *en route* to the hospital, that blood began to pour – from his nose first, then his ears. Soon after being admitted, he died.

'It has hit the village hard because we hadn't had an elephant death here for so long,' Asoka said. 'My grandchildren are frightened to even step outside the house. Even going outside to pick mango from our trees they are worried. We lived for so long without the electric fence, but in my small days, we were never this scared.' I wondered, then, what the ancient Sri Lankans, who built the great lakes and, perhaps unwittingly, facilitated the rampant spread of these jungles, would think of us now. In the twenty-first century, we had taken to fencing nature out, yet felt more besieged by wildlife than ever.

Two days later, I met an official from the Wildlife Authority in a nearby town. 'The thing you should never do when an elephant comes at you is run,' he said. 'Running encourages chasing, and over a short distance, an elephant will catch you and knock you down.' What you must do instead, he said, is stand your ground and shout because the elephant is most likely just making a 'mock charge' and will leave alone those it deems pose no threat.

I realized immediately that this was advice he was trained to give to tenacious rural types. City-bred pansies like me could never abide by this. Mock charge or not, there is as much chance of the elephant giving me a backrub as of me defiantly raising my voice to two-and-a-half tons of trumpeting grey fury closing in at forty kilometres an hour. I would be too frightened to even run. All actions would be involuntary. My best hope of survival would be to shit myself forcefully enough to launch my body to safety.

And what if it's not a mock charge? What if the elephant genuinely wishes to wear your skull like a roller skate? There are supposed clues that the elephant means business, like if it pins its ears back, or tucks in its trunk – but these aren't always reliable indications. The only sure-fire way to tell whether an elephant is mock charging or charging with intent is to stand your ground, then wait to see if you are killed or not. I could see why the influx of elephants made the Minneriya locals so nervous.

In the afternoon I caught two buses to the town of Medirigiriya in the hope of exploring the nearby ruins of a second-century Buddhist temple complex. The first leg of the journey was enlivened by loud conversation and laughter from the children who had just been let out of a local school. After I switched routes at Hingurakgoda, the jungle thinned out and paddy fields came back into view; their ripened crops heavy and golden-hued. Completing the pastoral scene were water buffaloes, half-submerged in roadside irrigation channels, birds pecking at their ticks.

There were less welcome sights on the journey as well. Sri Lanka had held its parliamentary elections two years prior, and the local MP's face was still all over the small towns and villages, including on large billboards thanking the public for their faith in him. On the corner of each of these billboards, the floating head of the party leader grinned maniacally at passersby.

This kind of showboating is a real menace in Sri Lanka. For starters, I'm not sure why politicians feel they must continually remind the public that they exist, because every time the power goes off, or the new road disintegrates with the first monsoon rains, politicians are widely and emphatically evoked, usually in sentences laden with curse words. People elected to office also love putting pictures of themselves near infrastructure projects completed during their tenure. Worse, they sometimes name the new buildings, roads, or power stations after themselves. There is a R. Premadasa Cricket Stadium in Colombo, for example, after the man who held presidential office in the early 1990s. The main airport is named for the Bandaranayakes – the island's most famous political family.

This seems odd to me. Overseeing additions to the nation's infrastructure is among the most basic obligations of any person in governance. Yet they feel they must constantly remind the public that it was them who delivered this progress, the insinuation being that development is an individual triumph – not one belonging to the state. No other professional demands this much attention for just doing their job. My barber doesn't attach a portrait of himself on the back of my head every time he gives me a haircut. Visits to the dentist don't end with grand inaugurations of the Dr Gooneratne Pre-Molar Filling. The rest of humanity collect our pay, take satisfaction from having helped provide goods or a service, and move on with our lives.

In the past decade, former president Mahinda Rajapakse made an art form out of political egotism. Even in non-election years, his face was plastered on most billboards, lamp posts, street signs, public-transport vehicles, tree trunks, abandoned buildings, mounds of dirt, and on posters hanging off strings clenched between the beaks of city crows. Getting lost at night in his home province in the south was a particularly galling experience. Every time you made a turn, your headlights would alarmingly find his brilliant smile and super-villain moustache. Forests of Rajapakse signboards obscured all identifiable landmarks. Sometimes it felt as if you would never find your way out of the dense plumes on his upper lip. Even now, so many months after Rajapakse's presidential ouster, I can more readily bring his visage to mind than the face of my own mother.

His successor, the bespectacled Maithripala Sirisena, has no moustache, but may well be remembered as one of history's great invertebrates. Since his election, Sirisena had careened from one political position to another, making enemies of old allies, friends of old opponents – a reed in a swamp, swaying pathetically in the direction of the prevailing political weather. Where Rajapakse had installed three brothers in high government positions, allowed his sons to flagrantly abuse state machinery, and generally moved Sri Lanka towards a family-run dictatorship, Sirisena had at first restored a measure of democracy, but had more-recently presided over a slowing economy, while the nation sat on the brink of avoidable crises. Contempt for the political class, as a result, was perhaps at an all-time high.

I disembarked at the Medirigiriya town centre around mid-afternoon with the impression the temple complex would be close by. As it turned out, I really should have just stayed on the bus. The man who gave me directions at the bus station suggested the complex was no more than a ten-minute amble in the same direction my bus had been travelling, but after half an hour of slogging through the heat, there was no sign of the temple.

It was only then that I remembered rural Sri Lankans have no talent for gauging distance. Almost everyone you meet in the provinces either substantially overestimates travel time or, more likely, spectacularly minimizes it. If someone tells you the place you are looking for is three kilometres to the east, for example, you may find it is just around the next bend. More likely, you will have to keep driving on and on, past vast tracts of paddy and scrub, over bridges, through deep glades until, at last, you reach your destination, somewhere in the southern regions of Japan.

Realizing I could still be miles off, I began looking around for a ride as I walked. By this stage even my clothes had sprung pores and were generating their own sweat. Not a single trishaw drove past, until finally, after the entrance to the ruins had come into view, no fewer than three puttered along, one after another, each slowing to ask me if I needed a ride. Why must it always be this way? There are never any taxis to be found when you would quite happily pay double, but when you decide you no longer need one, you have to climb past a mountain of them.

The temple complex was small but well preserved, the highlight being its raised, round shrine room (or *watadage*) most of whose three-dozen original 1,800-year-old stone pillars were still standing. The ancient statues of the Buddha, four in all and hewn from granite, were weathered but retained most of their parts and their beauty.

There are more impressive Buddhist ruins in the region, but perhaps none so tranquil. There were only two other visitors in the hour I was there. I climbed the rough-cut antique steps up towards the original stupa and spent much of my time there sitting on a dome-shaped granite rock, taking in a lotus pond below and the jungle just beyond it. Night fell as I made my way back to Habarana. Picking up my belongings there, I made a further forty-minute journey to a famous little town, one that takes its name from Sri Lanka's most popular tourist attraction.

Sigiriya's flies were holding their annual general meeting in the guesthouse verandah the next morning. Many of their number attempted to convene on the coconut roti and *lunu miris* – a paste made of onion, chilli and salt – I had been served for breakfast. Having spent a good twenty minutes flailing energetically at my food, I surrendered and let the meal go unfinished.

The flies were merely the latest of the challenges this establishment had presented. The previous evening, I had been ushered through a wood-imitation plastic door into a room about the size of a thimble. Inside, on top of a creaky wooden bed, was a mattress seemingly in a state of rigor mortis, unyielding bumps and joints projecting from its surface. This was covered by a tangle of unravelled thread, which at some point might have been a bedsheet.

The bathroom tap, also, was a piece of engineering unlike any I had encountered. It yielded a uniform dribble of water as I turned the handle four full rotations, then, upon the final quarter twist, unleashed a thunderous torrent, shooting streams along the curved porcelain sink to oblige me with a dramatic and unsolicited shower. When I eventually managed to wrestle the tap closed, waterfalls were cascading down the walls and galumphing raindrops were falling from the ceiling. The actual shower, meanwhile, produced no more than a grudging thread of moisture until you turned the handle so many times it came off in your hand. At this point the flow would cease completely.

One of Sri Lanka's engineering marvels: the faucet-shower combo.

But as I was paying only a thousand rupees a night here, I withheld my complaints from the owner, Chamee, whom I met on the verandah after breakfast. He was a tall man, big of belly, thick of jowl, gesturing animatedly, guffawing loudly, and smiling even more. Thrusting a cup of tea at me as I parked myself in a rattan-weave *haansi* chair, he told me he was a Sinhala and history teacher at the local high school. Chamee and his wife had only recently finished building the three-room guesthouse, which adjoined their own residence. They had wanted in on the tourism boom.

'You know, if two million foreigners come to Sri Lanka in a year, they say that at least two thirds will visit the Sigiriya rock fortress,' he told me in his forceful voice, throat all ajiggle. 'Small, small places like this are there all over the village now.'

In fact, all over the country, since the end of the war, small, small places such as these had opened their wood-imitation doors. They had begun to cater to a burgeoning quotient of budget tourists – mainly European couples, but also fresh-out-of-school teenagers on their 'gap year', and young families, on occasion. Wealthier hoteliers will call these places 'the informal sector', not without contempt for the smaller operators' flouting of planning laws and their periodic pressing of bribes into inspectors' fingers. But why shouldn't folks such as Chamee's family be carried along in the surge? Who could begrudge a rural schoolteacher the income?

And, anyway, are daily inconveniences not precisely the kind of authentic experience tourists slaver over? How cruel to preclude them from the dysfunction that flavours so much of Sri Lankan life. The mechanic will expertly replace the brake pads in your car, for example, but the moment you get the vehicle home, you will notice a trail of engine oil that could be followed all the way back to the garage. The electrician will install wall sockets neatly and efficiently but, following his visit, the television may only be turned on via the switch in the bathroom.

Later that morning, more homegrown mayhem was in evidence. At the entrance to the Sigiriya palace complex, there were two separate ticket offices. The one on the right had a crude sign that read, 'For foreigners', the queue beneath populated by genteel white folk and a couple of laidback East Asians, all equally spaced in ruler-straight single file. If so much as a backpack was unintentionally brushed, these people would launch into the most profuse, flowing apologies, chastising themselves for having been so careless.

To the left, however, was the almighty scrum in which I found myself. Dozens of Sri Lankans surged at once towards our ticket window, limbs tangled, ribcages compressed, cash-filled hands extended towards the harried cashier, and pained squawks filling the air. Strangely, it was the older folk who seemed to thrive in the scramble, perhaps by dint of experience. Spotting a small woman with greying hair next to me, I took care not to tread on her toes but, in a blink, she had elbowed four people in the spine and moved a metre closer to the window. On the opposite side of this whirl of bodies, a bald, whippet of a man had snatched the notes from the hand of his languishing daughter and, within seconds, ploughed his way to the front. This was not, by any means, an atypical Sri Lankan spectacle.

Orderly lines are liberally shunned at almost every level of society. Sometimes, if you deign to inform a latecomer that you had already been awaiting your turn at an ATM, for instance, they will click their tongues and roll their eyes, and generally act like the whole concept of queuing has just now been dreamt up to screw them over personally.

I was daubed with the sweat of a dozen strangers when eventually I emerged from the melee, but had in my clutches an inexpensive locals' entry ticket. It was worth the jostling. Foreigners may have their utopian queue but they pay close to seventy times as much. Yet happily do they flock to the rock.

The fortress of Sigiriya is a singular royal ruin in Sri Lanka. This is not merely down to its impressive size and spectacular location, but also a result of the peculiar ethos that produced it. Built in the fifth century by King Kasyapa, the palace that once stood atop the hulking granite monolith was ornate, showy, and plush – qualities largely at odds with the utilitarian ideals by which much of Sri Lanka's ancient period was defined.

If the palace is unique it is because – according to the island's *Culavamsa* chronicle – Kasyapa had himself been something of an iconoclast. An illegitimate son of the beloved King Dhatusena, the chronicle has Kasyapa seizing power through military coup, imprisoning his father, and driving his brother – the consecrated heir Moggalana – to India. Kasyapa would face no serious military challenge while his brother was abroad but nevertheless began to find himself harangued in what was then the capital: Anuradhapura. The city's powerful Buddhist clergy would not recognize a usurper. Nor, as a result, would the public readily accept his right to govern. Even in the earliest months of his reign, Kasyapa is understood to have grown increasingly bitter and paranoid.

In any case, he would soon make his rule in Anuradhapura untenable. Made to believe his father had hidden a great treasure, Kasyapa had dragged the old man out of jail, then demanded Dhatusena show him the loot. It is likely that the account is largely agenda-driven folklore, but the following, nevertheless, reveals a little about what was expected of a monarch of this period. Instead of leading his son to buried gold or hidden jewels, Dhatusena is said to have taken him to the Kalawewa Lake – supposedly the great irrigation project of his own reign – and declared his gift to his public the greatest treasure of his life. Kasyapa did not take well to this moralizing. Enraged, he had the old king killed, perhaps by having him entombed alive. Upon his return to Anuradhapura, Kasyapa found the city had begun to openly revile him. He made arrangements to move his court elsewhere.

Far to the southeast, amid thick jungle, the Sigiriya rock rose 212 metres, afforded a view of many miles, and had sheer cliffs on all four sides. Here not only was a position Kasyapa felt he could defend from Moggalana if the need ever arose, but one that also put seventy kilometres between himself and a religious establishment that would continue to revile him, despite many entreaties to the monks.

Unbound by Buddhism's moderating influence in this forest sanctuary, the king's appetites began to run unchecked. A man of sophistication and artistic sensibility despite his flaws, he commissioned magnificent sculptures for his palace, had frescoes painted on the exterior of the rock, built opulent bathing pools both at the crest of the monolith as well as at the lowest levels, and ordered the construction of audience halls, a reflective 'mirror wall', and a boulder arch along the western approach. Technologies that had been developed over centuries of irrigation-building were harnessed to produce sprawling fountain gardens largely pleasing to the eye and the ego.

The total effect is breathtaking. No grander royal residence had previously been seen in Lanka and perhaps not until Polonnaruwa's golden age, 700 years later, would Sigiriya's grandiose ambition be matched. Where the country's other capital cities were repeatedly sacked, Sigiriya, which had been the seat of power only during Kasyapa's eighteen-year reign, largely avoided war's ravages. Now, following twentieth-century excavations, it is wondrous again to behold.

Chamee, the guesthouse owner, had warned me about the gridlock. 'Why are you going to Sigiri on a Saturday morning?' he had bellowed. 'You will spend hours there just staring at other people's backsides. All the tour groups will be coming now.' Not wanting to fritter the morning away, however, I had ignored him, but sure enough, soon found myself repeatedly lodged within unmoving clots of humanity.

The busloads of locals and Chinese accounted for much of the blockage but delays on Sigiriya's staircases were not helped by tour guides, who would halt their groups at places of interest in order to pour forth to their clients. It was difficult to begrudge them, really. Theirs is not always dignified work. In the off-peak months, some guides will snatch an elbow and forcibly 'assist' older foreigners up the steps of the terraced gardens. Then they will mince around smiling until wallets are withdrawn and notes are handed over.

Among the highlights of the sweaty ascent were the last remaining frescoes, most of which are found in a cave about halfway up the rock. The paintings are of topless, slim-hipped women, appearing in a variety of poses: one counts the petals on a lotus, a column of bangles on her wrist; another supports a tray of fruits and flowers on her shoulder, filigreed golden crown rising from her hair. It is likely these are divine figures, or *apsara*s, but also possible that each portrait represented a royal consort. Traditionalist historians believe Kasyapa had maintained a vast harem – another excess believed to be typical of this king. Personally, I'd venture that the reason he needed so many concubines was because the women he chose were clearly all so top-heavy, they kept falling off the rock.

The final flight of steps had been entered through the mouth of a striking granite lion, of which only the flanking paws now remain. But at the summit, there was such a throng, nothing could be inspected or admired for long. The royal bathing pool was ringed with visitors: a little boy preparing to pee into the water before being stopped last moment, a clutch of teenagers almost tumbling backwards into the pool as they arranged themselves for a photograph. It was a potpourri of posing people up here. No buildings remained intact, only rock-hewn steps and brickwork bases.

The views over the surrounding landscape, however, were breathtaking. A carpet of forest stretched eastward, studded intermittently by twinkling lakes. The Pidurangala mountain, home to a still-functioning centuries-old monastery, stood to the north in its stately granite skullcap. Far to the south, the central mountains climbed out of the vegetation, and westward was the most fetching of the views: Sigiriya's fountain gardens in their long, handsome sprawl. For a minute, I stood on the edge of the rock and attempted to bring to mind the thousands who must have frolicked in the pools and water gardens during Kasyapa's years. How thrilling it must have been for his court to have been party to a royal project that took the gleanings from a millennium of urban settlement and turn them so unequivocally towards the extraction of pleasure.

But how wasteful his extravagance may have seemed to the larger populace. How despised he might have been, in an era whose monarchs were characterized chiefly by their civic works: their lakes, their channels, their temple complexes. When Kasyapa's brother Moggalana eventually returned to the island with an army, he gained the public's support, according to the *Culavamsa*, and routed Kasyapa's armies in the forests surrounding Sigiriya. Kasyapa's fate virtually sealed, he plunged his own sword into his belly, in 491 CE.

A little more than 1,600 years later, Sri Lanka had recently tossed out another set of preening rulers. The Rajapakses had once bestrode the south, beloved among the majority Sinhalese for having overseen the end of the war. But in the last few years of their rule, they began to be perceived as having overindulged. Many of their political allies had gained inordinate wealth, the president's sons had embarked on showboating public ventures such as sports channels and car races, and the rule of law was almost certainly bent out of shape to favour family loyalists. The Rajapakses remained a political powerhouse and had lately begun a dramatic resurgence – the profound failure of the present government paving their path back into power. But in their excess, at least once, they had triggered the public's gag reflex – a strain of which, perhaps, has been passed down from antiquity.

THREE

Up the Hill, into a Ditch

If you ever feel the need to have your private life disdainfully picked apart by a total stranger, do as I did and begin a conversation with a snarky person of middle-years on a Sri Lankan bus.

In fact, I had merely asked the lady if she would mind opening the shutter beside her, but to her, this was invitation enough. She pawed it open a minimum amount, so only the scantest wisps of fresh air squeaked through. Then, turning towards me, she unleashed a hurricane of prying questions.

'Where are you going?' and 'What are you doing there?' were innocent enough to begin with. But before I had finished replying, she had switched to 'Are you married?' territory, and from this there was no recovering. Within minutes she had crowbarred out details about my life: that my wife and I lived in Colombo, that we had been married five years, that we had no children as yet. Each answer was met with unsolicited commentary. Almost all of this was hostile.

Her: 'No children yet? Why? Something wrong?'

Me: 'No aunty, nothing like that. Well ... we just haven't ...'

Her: 'What is the point of being married if you haven't thought to raise children? Poor girl. No wonder she refuses to travel with you.'

Me [defensively]: 'No, she's actually got work during the week in Colombo.'

Her: 'Ah, so you are gallivanting around enjoying yourself and leaving your wife to earn the money, ah? Very nice.'

Me: 'Look, this is sort of work for me as well ...'

Her: 'In shorts and a T-shirt? Can imagine what kind of work you're doing.'

Coming to realize I would get no fair hearing, I decided to stop engaging. She, however, was not done with me yet. A sheen of pride suddenly added to her soaring condescension, she embarked upon a long monologue about her son.

'He is around your age only,' she insisted, but no, he would never dream of leaving his wife to go on a trip by himself. How could he travel solo, after all? He'd have to leave his two children: one three-year-old girl and a two-year-old boy, both such angels, and so clever – they have university written all over them. Did I want to see pictures? Well, why not if the photographs are right there in the envelope at the top of the handbag? Weren't they darlings? Did they not just make me want to change my mind about spawning offspring of my own? Was my life not hollow and inconsequential without cherubs such as these?

Most anywhere, perhaps it would have been strange for her to share family photographs with me, given the rancour that had developed between us. But when you are married and childless in Sri Lanka, this is what you come to expect. You make peace with the fact that you exist to be shown baby pictures, even by people who – as here – despise you. I suspect that from the moment I had asked her to open the window, she had set her mind on this endgame.

Thankfully I was soon rid of her when, having shot me a final sneer, she alighted. I slid into her seat, shoved the shutter until it came to a satisfying thud at the end of its rail, and, within moments, felt the unpleasantness of the last twenty minutes dissipate. The little ramshackle towns we were passing were curiously pretty: their banks housed in old colonial homes, their vegetable vendors peering out from behind bright produce, from beneath tumbledown tile roofs. As the bus had begun a mild ascent, the air here also felt cooler to the touch and fresher in my lungs; the blanket of lowland humidity having begun to loosen. I had, following a three-hour journey south from Sigiriya, begun to cut eastward towards the island's central hump.

That I had travelled so far out of my way to make a trip into the mountains was no surprise, I suppose, given that I was a coast-dweller. Lowland Sri Lankans fetishise the hill country; they adore its rolling peaks, its quaint architecture, its thunderous waterfalls. During the war years, those families that *did* venture Sri Lankan holidays seemed exclusively to visit the hill stations and, when friends had returned with boasts of the lip-smacking strawberries they had eaten and dairy farms on which the cows grew to the size of horses, it seemed, in those days, as if the hill country was almost another country. At the very least, it seemed like a place stuck in time.

But that was all to come. Before I entered the highlands proper, I still had one important detour to make. I disembarked at Mawanella, rode a trishaw on the ribbon road towards the village of Utuwankanda, and as the cries of children wielding rough-cut homemade cricket bats rang around the valley, the mountain of a childhood hero rose before us. It was hump-shaped and wooded, except for the granite outcrop in its highest reaches.

This had been the haunt of Sura Saradiel, Sri Lanka's beloved 1850s outlaw. He had watched over the Kandy road from the mountain and set his men about raiding merchant convoys that came along. In surrounding villages had lived the people who would hide and supply the gang – the folks with whom Saradiel had shared his life, and, so the story goes, his loot.

I had been drawn to the Saradiel picture book in the school library growing up. My friends, though, were obsessed with Robin Hood. A tall boy played Little John in our make-believe games. The leader of our little pack was usually Robin. Maybe it is because I was always stuck with playing the fat and pointless Friar Tuck that Sherwood Forest seemed to me a lesser magic; Utuwankanda is where I wanted to be.

The bandit's name was a first point of intrigue: Sa-ra-di-el – four musical syllables that leapt playfully off the tongue.

It was unlike any Sinhala name I had heard before, and that's because – I would later learn – it wasn't Sinhala at all. Saradiel's siblings were Gabriel, Pedro, Anthony, and Martha. Following two centuries of Portuguese and Dutch contact, and decades of British rule, the mid-nineteenth century found even the inland provinces in the colonists' cultural grip. Saradiel is not quite a European name, perhaps, but it was a Sri Lankan attempt at one.

Then there were the high-stakes hijinks. The folk stories have cast Saradiel as a saboteur of the British: his raids disrupting regional trade and his murders – all said to be committed in self-defence – acts of rebellion against oppressors of the common folk. But it was his wit that truly delighted. Once, while in remand, he had had an accomplice deliver his jailors a bottle of strong arrack, then made his break when the watchmen were intoxicated. (My Sinhala grandfather had been a career prison guard, yet he told this story with particular relish, taking great joy in admitting that he would have fallen for it himself.) On another occasion, when cops were closing in on Saradiel's hideout, he had the women in his village create a distraction, while he and his friends slipped into the jungle.

Small and fine featured himself, Saradiel appears to have had a productive relationship with women in general, reportedly sleeping with plenty in his time and often moving about the region in women's clothing, after the crown had put a £100 price on his capture and enlisted thousands of officers in the hunt. Historian W.M.K. Wijetunge recounts some of his more daring escapades:

> It is said that on one occasion he went in ladies' dress to a French play, at a theatre in Kurunegala, sat with the ladies and left a tell-tale engraving on the seat giving his name and the date of his visit.... On another visit to Kandy, wearing women's clothes, which were those of a woman of easy virtue, he went on his errand casting coy eyes on the constables he passed on the way. Next morning he delivered the same clothes to the police with his best compliments. The same modus operandi was repeated on another visit to Kandy, where he even engaged a policeman in a lively conversation, and returned the compliment by a gift of the incriminating apparel.

Beneath Saradiel's mountain now, a well-touristed model village has sprung up in the last decade. It was an attentive recreation, replete with life-size mudhouses, corner shops, a village temple, and even a toddy tavern – all decked out with period-appropriate furniture and implements. Detailed cement sculptures stood in for nineteenth-century villagers. Staff in costume greeted groups at the entrance. Once a reasonable price of admission was handed over, they guided visitors through the village. School groups and families with young children appeared to account for much of the patronage.

Sri Lanka very rarely brings its history to life with such care and creativity, so this place *should* have been a joy but, in fact, was a mild disappointment. I took the tour with a family from Kurunegala, who had arrived at roughly the same time. I was dismayed to find the history sold here was defanged. Our protagonist had been – slightly, but vitally – remoulded.

'Look at how eagerly young Saradiel bows to the temple monk,' our moustachioed guide beamed at a sculpture of a young boy paying obeisance with hands clasped above his head. 'You wonder if there are any children now who will worship like that.' Saradiel had been a Buddhist for all but the final days of his life, yet his religion was far from central to his story. In fact, the local monks are among the first authority figures Saradiel had run afoul of. His earliest assault had been on the wealthy son of a merchant who had mocked him and his poor friends during lessons at the temple. During his adolescence, Saradiel had also made off with a phial of valuable temple oil. On that, and other occasions, monks had supplied the information that occasioned Saradiel's arrests. They were in effect, stewards of one of the many establishments the outlaw spent his years defying.

Of Saradiel's skirmishes with the British, the tour offered a somewhat more truthful account. Colourfully retold was the story of his ambush of the Royal Mail, when Saradiel robbed the convoy and distributed the cash among underpaid government labourers. Further ahead, a sculpture of Saradiel upon horseback anchored the story about his winning over of a fearful village by tossing out cash as he rode through, proclaiming himself 'a friend to the poor'.

Glossed over, however, were the details of the company he kept. Mammalai Marikkar, his right-hand man, was a Muslim, as was Menaka-Menaka, his favourite mistress. Saradiel had been at her house when police found and arrested him for the final time. That he had been betrayed by a Sinhala accomplice, and that he had converted to Christianity in jail, also went untold.

In truth, he had been a pan-Sri Lankan hero. Yet, it is unsurprising that his race and religion were so emphatically invoked here: in post-Independence Sri Lanka, history that fails to assert Sinhala-Buddhist primacy is often no history at all.

As the sun began to descend, I left the model village, and set out to climb the Utuwankanda hill with the family I had accompanied on the tour. It was a challenging ascent in parts. We pulled each other up over the big boulders and took turns carrying their toddler up the slippery gravel slopes. I fell over repeatedly, grazing my arms on the rocky bits and skinning one knee. When we reached the lookout at the top, a group of university students beckoned us over and passed around the bread, *katta sambol* (a spicy paste made of flakes of dried fish and onion), and bananas they had carried up. The forest stretched out in an undulating carpet below. The central highlands brooded in the distance.

The tamasha at the foot of his mountain may not have been completely truthful. But through favours done and a small meal shared, at the summit of his mountain, the spirit of Saradiel was honoured.

Foreign couples canoodled on lakeside benches while macaque monkeys rifled through their backpacks, trishaws tore down hillside roads like they were being pursued by Raiders-of-the-Lost-Ark boulders, a billion bakeries stood on the main drag, flower-sellers hawked on the corners; I had arrived, unmistakably, in Kandy.

The proper welcome here for a Colombo resident such as myself is to be spat in the face by a local. Kandyans are better than us lowland types, because (*a*) they had resisted colonialism for three full centuries longer than the cowards on the coast, (*b*) they'd clung on to their traditional religion and family names unlike my spineless ancestors, and (*c*) their city was a whole 500 metres higher, and, as such, a few degrees cooler than the hellish, crime-ridden, sweat festival that was the capital.

The ninety-minute bus ride in from Utuwankanda had been uneventful, though, it must be said, that is only by the standards of this particular road. The A1 – which wends its way through the hills between Colombo and Kandy – is governed by an unusual law, which is that all vehicles must, at all times, seek to overtake all other vehicles, even those travelling in the opposite direction, if possible.

The result is a messy and slow-moving potpourri of metal. Lorries piled with coconut hold up long queues of cars. Trishaws wedge themselves in the path of furious public buses. Vans that have finally disentangled themselves from one snarl of traffic are brought to immediate, screeching stops by pedestrians flitting carelessly across the tarmac. Every few months, when a vehicle tumbles down a hillside into a river, the Transport Authority will proclaim it a tragic 'accident'. Those who have driven the A1, and are familiar with the hopeless rage it inspires, may have their doubts.

Arriving in Kandy without incident pleased me twofold on

this occasion because, after weeks of inexpensive rooms with mattresses no thicker than sheets of corrugated iron and about as comfortable, I had booked myself three nights of opulence. A plush new hotel lay waiting for me in the higher reaches of a hill in the northern suburbs. The reason for the upgrade: Erena was coming for a two-day stay. Or, at least, I told myself that was why.

And what a visit it turned out to be. She came in on an evening bus from Colombo and the next morning we set about indulging in all the clichéd Kandy pleasures. We strolled around the town's pretty central lake and found a little time to read on the banks – a gaggle of Muscovy ducks for company. We traipsed through the markets and ate at the bakeries. We had coffee at the unforgettably garish Helga's Folly Chalet, then dined and drank some more at an open-air pub that overlooked the town and lake. The Temple of the Tooth got its customary visit.

This was all when we could tear ourselves away from the hotel, which afforded a cumulus cloud of luxurious bedding, a vast breakfast spread of hoppers, curries, sambols and bread, and ravishing views over the impossibly verdant Knuckles mountain range. On the second day, Erena even spent so long at the stunning rooftop pool that we needn't have bothered switching on the lights after nightfall, so resplendently did our lodgings glow by the light of her sunburned radiance.

I felt obscenely pampered. I slept too long, ate too much good food, drank too much arrack, and took far too much delight in rich-person excesses such as taking long, hot showers, then ratcheting up the air conditioning to cool myself down. But all this, alas, could not last. Erena's leave came to an end and she bade me goodbye to catch the early morning train back to Colombo. Later that day, I dragged myself and a backpack full of freshly laundered clothes out of the hotel, into a trishaw, and back into another corrugated-iron-mattressed room. The real world would receive me with quite a bump.

'Any form of artistic expression that has survived in Sinhala society today, owes its origin to, or has derived inspiration from, Kandy,' writes historian Lorna Devaraja. Well, it does seem almost indisputable.

Look in on any traditional Sinhala wedding. The groom wears the glittering square cap and ornately embroidered jacket that is the customary attire of the Nilame, or steward of Kandy's Temple of the Tooth. At the homecoming event – itself a wedding tradition with Kandyan roots – the woman drapes her sari with a small fount of pleats emerging from the left hip, in the Kandyan *osiri* style. Kandyan drummers will also often play the newlyweds out of their *poruwa* ceremony, with hill-country dancers leading the way.

In addition, Kandy's Esala Perehara attracts the largest audience of any Buddhist festival, the Temple of the Tooth is the most-visited religious site on the island, and the sword-wielding lion on the national flag is derived directly from the banners of the last Kandyan kings.

The hill capital presents itself as the shining store of Sinhala heritage because, where three additional centuries of colonialism are believed to have ravaged lowland culture, in Kandy is thought to have been preserved a concentrated nub of ethnic identity. People look here for a blueprint of tradition – authenticity flowing down from altitude, like so many rivers to the coasts.

And as it is this high-seat of Buddhism, there is also the notion that Kandy must necessarily be a reserved and pious place. Try finding a good meal in the city after 10 pm, for instance; only the franchise pizza joints really stay open, and even they are often shut an hour later. Or attempt to settle down at a bar late in the evening. Perhaps the only joint that will serve you is 'The Pub' – so called presumably because for much of its existence, it was the only establishment of its kind in town. The tourism boom has perhaps recently bestowed some semblance of a nightlife upon the town but temperance and conservatism remain the overwhelming themes.

Yet, Kandy has not always been so stereotypically straight laced.

Writing in 1803 – twelve years before Kandy fell to the British – Captain Robert Percival of the British 19th Foot Regiment describes unrecognizable attitudes towards sex and marital affairs, though with the colossal condescension of an Empire-builder.

'A Cinglese husband is not in the smallest degree jealous of his wife, and is rather ambitious about displaying her to the public eye, nor is he particularly offended at her infidelity to him …' he writes in *Account of the Island Ceylon*. 'The infringement of chastity scarcely subjects a woman either married or unmarried to the slightest reproach, unless indeed they happen to have connexion with one of a lower cast … among the Candians in particular, this one distinction of moral turpitude, which is so worthy of a barbarous nation, is carried to the highest pitch.'

I would like to interject here to remind the Captain that even decades after he bloviated so severely about Kandyan barbarity, back in England, the likes of Oliver Twist were having their sweet little orphan buttocks furiously reddened by workhouse canes. But I digress; he goes on …

'With people of their own rank, on the contrary, the most unbounded commerce is carried on in private; and it is by no means uncommon, nor attended with any disgrace, for the nearest relations to have connexion with each other.'

Promiscuity had in fact been a feature of Kandyan society long before the nineteenth century. In his famous account of captivity in Kandy between 1660 and 1680, British sailor Robert Knox had also been struck by the local appetite for carnal adventure.

'There is nothing so common as whoredom, so that youth are bred up to whoredom,' he writes of Kandyans. 'The woman reckons herself as much obliged to the man for his company, as he does to her for hers. In [extramarital] affairs, the women are very expert (it being their continual practice) to keep their design from the husband's knowledge: though by his own experience he cannot be ignorant of women's devices. And unless he catch them in the act, he doth not much trouble himself to prove himself a cuckold; cuckolds being so common, that it is not here regarded.'

How attitudes have flipped. Following British conquest, sexual norms became warped and the island recast its historically liberal Buddhist tradition in a brooding, conservative vein. Where women once went bare-breasted in public, for example, there are now high schools that frown on mothers wearing sleeveless tops when they drop off children. Where it once was natural for prospective spouses to cohabit before marriage, present-day parents who so much as suspect their offspring are engaged in sexual relationships will, at the very least, set such children on fire.

This adopted conservatism has led to all sorts of strange social phenomena, among them: young couples choosing to rendezvous in odd places in order to confound parental surveillance. Of this I was irritatingly reminded that day.

I had set out for the municipal library with the aim of gaining a better grip on the hill country's history. Maybe it was because I was still grieving the loss of my wife's company and the absence of our hotel extravagances that I didn't fancy the hike in the Knuckles range I had planned for the day. No, I thought. The yellowing volumes of the reference section and its ancient wooden desks would do nicely instead. I arrived mid-afternoon, picked out a few promising books, and sat down beneath a dusty ceiling fan. Only a few minutes passed before a teenaged couple arrived. Settling at a desk a few metres to my right, they began to shower their surroundings with unholy torrents of pent up hormones.

It was unbearable. Though they drew serious-looking textbooks and note-filled binders from their bags to suggest they were here to study, within minutes, what started as a murmur between them developed into annoying tittering, and then full-blown, full-throated nonsense. The young man – tall and slender, but with front teeth like a mole rat – cracked increasingly loud and gormless jokes. His companion – who emitted sounds exclusively through her nose – snorted endlessly at each one. At her encouragement, he would also join in with monotone guffaws. When some couples laugh together, they can make the world feel full of light and music. These two sounded like a flock of ducks being shot at.

Then the touching began. He poked her in the ribs until she squealed. She delivered playful slaps across his shoulder. Soon, hands were rubbing on thighs, fingers were intertwining, and arms were being wrapped around waists. I tried intently to dive into a history of the Uva rebellion for a few minutes but, eurgh, what was that noise? Was it ... a moan? When I looked up, she was stroking his hair like she was trying to bring his follicles to orgasm.

Normally, a librarian would arrive to shut them up, or better yet, eject them, but sadly none were stationed in the room that day. In fact, the only time I saw a staff member was when one miraculously appeared just outside the door to tell *me* off for trying to escape to a different room with reference books. 'If you aren't going to let me go elsewhere, please come in and put an end to the pheromone festival,' I pleaded, though perhaps in not as many words. Instead, she clicked her tongue and harrumphed at me for having dared to suggest she make herself mildly useful. When I re-entered, the couple looked like they had been nuzzling on each other's necks. The room seemed more full of sexual frustration than of books or air.

Afraid of vomiting all over my reading, I abandoned it and left.

Who was I to blame really? Perhaps I should have confronted them myself, but in the back of my mind was the thought that none of this was their fault. This is just what people in their late teens did. In pre-British Kandy, this fellow might be disappointing his girlfriend in the corner of a mud-brick home, somewhere out of sight. In many other nations, they would be spreading their DNA over a threadbare couch, or on a seedy motel bed. Instead, they probably had the kinds of parents who would follow them right to the library doorstep, just to ensure they were up to no mischief. Cornered thus by convention, perhaps they had just decided to glean what thrills they could in the quietest room in the building. I was merely collateral.

At any rate, that Tuesday would get much worse. Having learned precious little about hill country history in the library, I picked up a book at a store, and in the evening, pitched up to a hillside bar to look through it. In evidence at the bar was more sexual ambition: two Kandyan men schmoozed around the room, laying on foreign women lines like: 'Sri Lankan girls are not that much into having fun, like Europeans,' and 'Ah, you're from England? I had the best night of my life with an English girl.' They struck out the first few times, but perhaps, against all odds, they got lucky later on. I couldn't really say. I spent much of the evening reading and only when the waiter produced my bill unprompted did I realize I must have spent much of it downing arrack as well. The opposite wall throbbed at me as I paid up. The earth wobbled inconsiderately as I strode, swaying, out of the bar and clambered into a trishaw. I had spent many sober evenings on this trip, almost all of which were uneventful. The universe chose this particular one to deliver the major mishap of the journey.

It happened as we were shooting along one of those unlit, downhill stretches that Kandy seems to specialize in. The driver I was with seemed a decent fellow but, as with many young trishaw drivers in the country, also enjoyed gleaning every last iota of thrust his four-stroke engine would offer him. This would still have been fine had we not also encountered a true moron of the streets. As we rounded a bend, a rival trishaw materialized suddenly in our lane, its headlights blazing like a bonfire, its little tires devouring the road between us with malicious intent. My driver twisted sharply to the right, avoiding the gravest danger, but was met with defiant screeches of rubber as he strove to correct course. The other trishaw sped past us, but we skidded. We fishtailed. Then we teetered. We swore in at least two languages, and at some point, we toppled over. It was at this moment that my face had its brief but emphatic meeting with the vehicle's steel side bar, while a clod of soil also launched itself into my mouth. When, a little dazed, we tumbled out onto the road, the trishaw lay almost peacefully in a broad ditch. Tranquillity had suddenly reclaimed the street. The other vehicle had disappeared as abruptly as it had come into view.

Of the evening's subsequent events, only snatches remain to my recollection, maybe because of the blow I had suffered, or perhaps because of my alcohol-addled state. I remember my driver worriedly slapping his forehead when he discovered the gash in mine – the dark splotches on my green shirt growing larger, warmer and wetter on account

Mid-tumble, swearing in multiple languages, about to eat dirt.

of the trickle flowing down my nose. I remember a passing trishaw being waved down and then my being transported to Kandy's general hospital, where a staggeringly unhelpful nurse told me the doctors were busy, and a hospital policeman kept accosting me with some kind of form. I remember cutting my losses at this institution and instead paying to be treated at a private clinic, where after repeatedly having to swear to another nurse that I had not been beaten up, she kept insisting to the doctor that I must have been in a gang fight. And I remember the doctor misfiring the local anaesthetic injection through my scalp and, soon after, the sting of the needle tearing its way through five stitches. The rest of the night was a haze.

When I awoke sober and sore in my guesthouse room the next morning, there were two further revelations. The first, thanks to a still-ringing left ear, was that I had managed to rupture an eardrum in the collision (an injury that would thankfully heal, in time). The second, courtesy of a rummage through my wallet, was that the trishaw driver who had ferried me to two hospitals, sat in the waiting room while I was treated, and then returned me to my lodgings, had not taken a cent for his troubles. Later in the morning he would even call me to ask how I was doing, having pried my number from my ailing mind during the ordeal.

'How could I accept money from you when you are facing so much trouble?' he asked. 'Did you see how much the clinic anyway charged from your card? No heart, you know? No humanity, these people.'

Like the stay in Kandy, the night had been a showcase of the nation's extremes. If you catch Sri Lanka in one of her manic, self-sabotaging moods, she will relentlessly screw you over; her establishments will deliver kicks to the gut, thumb their nose at you, and pick your pocket when you are unconscious. But in her own fashion, the island almost always finds a way of redeeming herself, even if only partially, but in the most unlikely and warming ways.

I was surprised to find it was the good that made the deeper impression. When my fingertips ran over my scar during the remainder of my travels, it's not the ridiculous driving I thought of, or the maddening hospital bureaucracy, or even the medical incompetence. It was the kindness of a man whose vehicle I must have bled on, whose face I can't bring to mind, and whose name, to my regret, I never learned.

FOUR

The White and the Black–White

I must have been quite a sight on the train further east to Nuwara Eliya. On top of the untidy stitches on my forehead, I was limping on account of a banged-up big toe (another delayed revelation), I had begun to wincingly cock my head to the left whenever my ear hurt, the scabs on my arms from the climb up Utuwankanda had not yet healed, and there was always the birthmark on my forehead, which kids at school used to say looked like God had taken a little dump on my face.

To the untrained eye, I must have looked vaguely leprous. But instead of steering clear of me, fellow passengers helped me pack my bag into an already overflowing overhead compartment and one fellow even briefly disembarked at a station to buy me a bottle of water after I had casually complained I was thirsty.

While I rested my hideous face on the windowpane, the hill country beamed its enchanting landscapes back at me. Runnels of white water warbled beneath the rail bridges, then flung themselves off cliffs to become lost in the valleys. Great forests of pines enclosed us with dark, wet trunks – their needles clashing with the deep red of carriages. Higher up, hill country women plucked tips between rolling rows of tea, vermilion flame-of-the-forest canopies lit up the distance, and wildflowers spangled beside the railroad.

If the Himalayas left the visitor awestruck and breathless, here were mountain views to soothe the soul. I mean, who could have failed to be cheered by clumps of waving children as the train wended its way past a schoolyard? Who could have resisted the charms of the narrow hillside paths and the little houses with vegetable plots that sprung suddenly up inside wooded glades? After the twenty-four hours I had had, these things almost moved this sappy dolt to tears.

The scent of petrichor grew heavier the further we ascended, and soon my carriage-mates began to retrieve their bags from the shelves to fish out jumpers and cardigans. The train rested briefly at Hatton station to allow an oncoming one to pass. When we pushed off again the views became evermore scenic. Colonial bungalows sat primly near the ridge, surveying wide sweeps of tea. In the valleys squatted the factories, sunlight glinting off their metallic sheeting. Whatever else you may think about British interference in South Asia, on creating landscapes as pretty as they were profitable, the pricks did seem to know a thing or two. On their own island, the likes of the Yorkshire Dales are intensively farmed, yet remain undeniably enchanting – the paddocks bounded by those mottled stone walls, sheep speckling hillsides. Here, the tea industry is a vital contributor to the manufacturing economy and has the added benefit of drawing tourism to the region.

That is not to say, of course, that nothing was lost in the making of these estates. Writing in 1930, British adventurer John Still describes the last of the tracts of towering native forest that had reigned over some of these hills before the colonists felled them.

> Here and there on the hill-tops prudent planters had left small patches of ancient woods untouched as timber reserves, whose most interesting function was to offer a last refuge to a few wild animals.... Wild pigs were to be found in them, and families of the deep-voiced wanderoo monkeys; and of the deer tribe the little muntjac was common, and even the great sambhur, as large as a pony, not unknown.

Still was something of an environmentalist (which for an early twentieth-century British man means he killed hundreds upon hundreds of rare animals for sport, but had the sense to feel bad about it later in life) and an uninhibited writer on even the commonest natural landscapes. He is especially impassioned when he dwells on the destruction wrought by colonial agriculture.

> Towering forms of age-old trees stood like giants looking out over scores of miles of hills and valleys once the home of ten thousand of their kind, but now given over to tea, a humble white-flowering camellia, precious to man the

destroyer, grown in neat rows. In these rare woods jungle fowl abounded; and beautiful rose-coloured begonias, red and white balsams, tree ferns and orchids made lovely their dim recesses where the streams sang their songs of the ages and ran down to turn turbines in the valley far below.

If Still was so moved in the early decades of the twentieth century, he might be positively suicidal if he learnt what had happened to Sri Lanka's forests since. The British had stripped the island of about forty per cent of its native woodland in roughly 150 years of occupation, but about as much again has been removed since their departure. Each year perhaps 30,000 hectares – an area about half the size of Colombo – falls to the saw to make way for farmland. Sri Lanka's population has remained roughly stable for the past twenty years, but its appetite, like its economy, has expanded.

As lovely as the views were, my injuries and fatigue soon began to wear me down. My forehead throbbed, the bones in my foot ached, and nausea came in nasty little spells. When the train eventually pulled into Nanu Oya, I disembarked, took a trishaw to Nuwara Eliya, and stumbled into the first guesthouse I could find. I collapsed into bed.

Maybe it was because I had felt so unwell that I thought of my Tamil grandmother when I awoke. At times in our childhood, she had been sort of a de facto nurse to my sisters and me. Whenever we fell sick my mother would ferry us all to my grandmother's place, in the belief her seaside home was better suited to our recovery than our dusty one. Very quickly, however, these visits began to fill me with dread. This is because, although doting, generous, and good-humoured in most respects, my grandmother was also one of Earth's greatest hypochondriacs.

She was a wonder to behold when she felt her grandchildren in peril. Armed even at the best of times with some ointment or herbal drink, our arrival would send her into an organizational frenzy. Blankets smelling of mothballs were withdrawn from wardrobes, wash cloths for the mopping of foreheads were neatly laid out on bedroom dressers, Catholic prayer books were dusted off, and her rosary was constantly fingered. Soon she would begin readying her arsenal of medicines like a nation preparing for a protracted war. One by one, these would be visited upon us.

The first mode of attack was usually something called Eau de Cologne. This came in a dimpled glass bottle and was a clear sweet-smelling liquid that she would rub through our scalps every few hours. Though no more than a low-end fragrance produced by the Johnson & Johnson company, Eau de Cologne had become a favoured remedy of many South Asians of her era, and my grandmother's faith in it was total. In her imagination, it staved off fevers, fought colds, busted headaches, alleviated swelling, cleared the sinuses, and would have brought gravely wounded soldiers to perfect health had generals ever had the sense to aerially spray battlefields with the stuff.

When the Eau de Cologne inevitably failed to cure us, we were brusquely told we must have been struck down with an especially stubborn illness as punishment for our disobedience and, before long, the traumatic steam inhalations would commence. For these she boiled up a few garden leaves in a large steel pot until the concoction had turned a bubbling, grey-green. She then had us breathe its fumes, standing over the brew with bedsheets over our heads, lest the precious healing vapours escape. I would always emerge from beneath the sheet feeling nauseated. If this were to progress to vomiting, my grandmother would declare it a clear sign that one inhalation had been inadequate and I would be shuffled over to the stove and have a bedsheet thrown over my head again.

On our diet, my grandmother was especially particular. At mealtimes my sisters and I subsisted largely on *kola kenda* – a sort of cold soup, which looked and tasted like blended grass. This was followed by a drink called *kasaaya*, which I am certain receives a mention in the UN's charter on human torture. My mother, bless her, tried on occasion to convince our grandmother to feed us some carbohydrates or protein. These appeals were rarely of use. My grandmother was queen in her own home and any challenge to her medical regimen was met unfailingly with sharp invective. Throughout our stay she would also ban bananas, pineapples, papaya, *thambili* or cucumber, because her longtime physician Dr Ratnasiri had told her that these were 'cooling foods' that weakened the immune system. In fact, during times of illness, Dr Ratnasiri would be invoked almost as many times as Jesus, Mary, and the Saints, which was saying a lot. It was only later in life that I learned the great doctor had actually died long before I was born – probably of the sniffles, going by the quality of the advice he had furnished his patients with.

In any case, my grandmother would have berated me endlessly if she could have seen my state after the accident. 'Why were you traveling so late at night like a vagabond, ah?' she would have demanded. 'After everything your parents have done to bring you up, can't you live decently?' No doubt she would have insisted I cut the trip short, and return home immediately, preferably by helicopter-ambulance. She would also have been especially cross if she had seen me step out into Nuwara Eliya's early evening wearing only two layers. But in maintaining this deathly fear of the cold, at least, she was merely like most low-country Sri Lankans.

Even on that first walk through town, it was almost immediately obvious which Sri Lankans were visitors from the coasts and which were locals. While Nuwara Eliya residents wore one jumper and maybe a woollen hat in temperatures that were still in the high teens, low-country folk had come attired for an expedition to the Antarctic. There were whole groups buried beneath piles of thick fabric – a vast stratum of jumpers propping up stiff arms like the limbs of marionettes, their heads swaddled in colourful beanies, their torsos so well encased a rifle shot to the belly might have failed to pierce the skin. The children were so comically spherical in this get-up, I was constantly fighting the urge to push them over to see how fast they would roll down the hills.

Nuwara Eliya is a favoured destination among Sri Lankans, partly because they can come here to pretend they are visiting a Western nation. The town itself did truly feel like knock-off piece of Britain at times. Fake Tudor-architecture abounded about the fringes of the city and the streets still had names like Queen Elizabeth Drive, or Mountmary Road, all studded with guest-house cottages going by Glendower or Albany or King Fern or Queenswood or Grosvenor. It is likely some of those establishments had accommodated the British here, the colonists themselves having made a custom of holidaying in the hills in order to escape lowland heat.

Occasionally, the British vestiges even gave the place a little charm. The grand, red-brick post office posturing magisterially over a major intersection is among the most striking public buildings in the country, while the pristine golf course, Victoria Park, and the recently-refurbished racecourse provide Nuwara Eliya with the orderly wide-open spaces that always seem to be in shortage in other Sri Lankan towns.

That evening, having bought myself a few warm clothes to get me through the week, I dined at a hotel in whose corridors hung black-and-white photographs of eminent hill country planters, whose staff were dressed in colonial livery and whose commitment to its theme was so comprehensive that the roast beef I was served tasted like it had been prepared in 1935.

But as I ate, Nuwara Eliya's colonial schtick did strike me as somewhat ironic. Before tea took over the surrounding country, before prim homes with brick chimney stacks and old-timey gables perched up on the hills – before Nuwara Eliya became the Sri Lankan Simla – these parts had given birth to a rebellion. It was in the hills in 1817 that the greatest military challenge to British power had risen up.

The Uva province chieftain who led the war was Keppetipola Disawe. There is a little bickering among historians about his exact motivations in the conflict, but on one point most agree: it was at his joining that the resistance acquired the gravitas that transformed it from a local uprising to bona fide rebellion.

That Keppetipola joined it at all represented something of a reversal, since he had been among the hill country nobles who in 1815 had signed over the Kandyan territories to the British. In fact, various aristocratic families had been plotting to depose the Kandyan monarchy on-and-off for more than a century, conspiring at first with the Dutch before the British arrived with sufficient muscle to overrun the hills and force the issue. Yet, two years after the king was evicted, the clutches of these nobles were, like men who had invited in snakes to rid themselves of the rats, waging battle against the new pests.

It is important here to note that aristocratic dissension with the monarch was never shared by the common people. The public was not especially enamoured of the final Kandyan king, perhaps, but they had hardly shown a desire to dethrone him. The stronger inclination among commoners was their deep-seated distrust of foreign rule. Once the nobles eventually came around to resenting the British, largely because Buddhist customs had become besieged, the public's long-standing tradition of resistance served as political tinder. Within the space of a few weeks, flint struck metal, sparks shot across the mountains, and the fire of rebellion spread.

The insurgency would eventually turn out to be traumatic for the people of Uva, but there was, in the first months at least, a little success. Keppetipola's defection had caught the British largely unawares and his guerilla attacks were consequently instrumental in making early ground on thinly-spread colonial forces. When the monsoon arrived to swell rivers and stymie inland communication, the British grip on the hills loosened further.

Marshalling the troops of the Empire, however, was Robert Brownrigg, a hardened soldier though, crucially, a man with no experience in civil administration before his term as Governor. Brownrigg sent fevered letters demanding reinforcements from colleagues in South Asia but, in the meantime, sought to crush the rebellion with chilling barbarity. He ordered a campaign of scorched-earth terror upon the mutinous provinces: if he could not crush the insurgents in battle with the forces that remained in his command, Brownrigg sought to demoralize rebel bastions; if he could not capture the chiefs, he would torch their supplies and cut off recruitment at the source.

It was this British savagery that had devastated the village of Paranagama in early 1818, though you could never tell if you travelled there now. The next day, I rode a bus east to the town of Welimada, then took a trishaw north, into narrower roads. Even for a mountain village, Paranagama was unusually pretty: its houses fronted by neatly terraced vegetable plots, its creeks of cool, clear water forever babbling nearby. Set deep in a valley, pine and turpentine forests trimmed the higher reaches of the surrounding mountains while yellow bursts of *kaha kona* bloom enlivened the lower slopes. On the air came familiar agricultural scents: whiffs of wet hay and dried manure. Half-broken bullock carts lay in distant fields. Shiny landmasters sat in dirt driveways.

I had come here in search of a site of particular British cruelty, known as the *wadaka gaha*, or torture tree. Not many English history books have paid it much attention but mentions of it are littered through Sinhala histories of the rebellion. Some sources claim only Paranagama men of fighting age were lynched from the tall tamarind tree that had stood near the centre of the village. Others suggest boys as young as fourteen and many women were also strung up.

It took some finding. I had read the tree now stood within the grounds of a village school, but the teachers at the first college we came upon furrowed their brows and shrugged. What tree?

Having weaved around the village and stopping several times for directions, I found it, eventually, at a smaller school. It stood tall and healthy still, almost 200 years later, the tough charcoal bark at its base giving out to lighter shades of brown near the high branches. We had had to have it pointed out to us because there was no plaque or memorial to mark it out. In fact, the only indication to its historical significance had been left by the British themselves: the crumbling foundations of a small brick fort they had built, lying metres away.

This was very unsatisfying. I had hoped the tree would be

shrouded in stories of the rebellion, or at the very least, tales of people who died at the site. I had thought I could discover a little more about the particular horrors that war had brought to this village. But everyone I met near the tree seemed to have no more information than myself, even if they did, bless them, try their best to make themselves helpful. One teacher pointed to branches and suggested that was where the ropes for lynching might have gone, as if he was blowing a great mystery wide open for me. The war must have been very unpleasant, another woman remarked.

I had almost resigned myself to returning to my lodgings, but it was at this point that the trishaw driver salvaged the expedition, having developed a little academic enthusiasm himself. 'We should try the temples,' he announced, working off the theory that village monks have traditionally been founts of local information. Almost before I could respond, he had already pulled into a temple that happened to adjoin the school, leapt out of his vehicle, and strode over to the monk to prostrate himself at his feet.

The monk turned out to be no more knowledgeable than the villagers and soon we were off again, looking for another temple. We were rebuffed a second time by a younger bhikku who emerged from his quarters rubbing his eyes, to tell us the chief monk was away in Colombo.

'See, this is the problem with our monks these days,' the driver seethed as we pulled away again.

'What do you mean?' I asked.

'They had nothing for you, no? If they don't know about the village history, then who would?'

'Maybe they're not from around here.'

'That's not the point. In my small days, the monks in a village made it a point to know the stories of the people they were serving.'

'And now?'

'Now? *Aiyo*, no point even talking about it. Now they will get their alms from the people in the morning, have a good lunch, and then just go to sleep. Tell me if you can – what good is that to anyone?'

We came upon a third village temple and this time even I knelt at the monk's feet wondering if this would be the key to jogging his memory. I need not have bothered – this monk was unlike the others. A learned and serious man, he threw the end of his robes over his shoulder and sat us down on a bench in the temple verandah. Folding himself a fat wad of betel, he began to pour forth. The details came in a torrent.

It was because of Paranagama's geographical position that the village had been a particular flashpoint during the rebellion, he said. Situated on the road between British-controlled Kandy and the Uva capital of Badulla, this had been one of the first major outposts in rebel territory. The British had killed as much as half the village's population but had also set the fields alight and torn down most homes.

He told tales of harrowing privation. Old men had been slapped in stocks and left in the woods to starve or be killed by animals – their punishment for refusing to reveal rebel whereabouts. Village leaders had been slain first as an example to the others, women were abused, then forced to feed the

British soldiers. Many families abandoned ancestral lands and fled south, into the jungle.

I wondered how much of this oral history had been embellished over time but the war had inscribed itself indelibly on the village by other means. Less than a kilometre away from this temple, for example, a terraced stretch of paddies had been known since the rebellion as Lekumbura, the field of blood. Also nearby was Atubediella – a waterfall at the foot of which rebel grain supplies used to be stored. At the forest clearing of Atampitiya – a bastardization of the word that translates to 'battleground' – local militia are said to have trained.

In the sudden warmth that overtook the mountain chill that afternoon, the monk took us along as he went to bathe in a creek that ran alongside Atampitiya. On the way we met a friend of his, a farmer by the name of Cyril Jothipala who had dark, sloth-bear forearms, a flourishing moustache, and a smouldering anger at the British, as if the rebellion had ended only months ago.

'Did you know, one of the descendants of the major MacDonald who built that fort in the school had come here some time back?' Jothipala asked, incredulous. 'Can you imagine? After what they did to us, he is coming proudly to see his great grandfather's work. Lucky for him I wasn't there. I would have chased him off like anything.'

As the monk bathed behind a screen of tall grass, we sat on the banks of the creek listening to Jothipala's grouses. He delivered these standing above us, like a preacher with his congregation. He lamented the pines that the British had introduced to the mountaintops. 'They don't retain any water unlike our endemic trees. Now every drop of rain flows downhill before we have a chance to make use of it.' He maligned the governance model Sri Lanka had inherited after independence. 'If we had had a chance to shape politics on our own, we could have actually come up with something that suits this country.' Most of all, though, he raged about the tea industry and the exploitation of labour that is hardcoded into its practices. 'Go to some of the labourers' line rooms while you're in the hill country,' he said. 'See the way they have been treated through history. Then you will understand about the British. Then you will see how great they were.'

Of the 'Skeleton Road' from Mannar to the hill country, a British planter had written in the 1840s that 'one could fill two carts with the skulls of those who have been abandoned, unburied'. The skulls belonged to migrants. Believing the Sinhalese too indolent for work on their newly made estates, the British had coaxed to the island gangs of men from Tamil Nadu, which (thanks to economic decline in that region for which the British had themselves been catalysts) had become a sort of cache of imperial labour. Though the workers had been led to believe the island abounded with opportunity, they found upon making shore that a 150-kilometre trek through dry scrub and jungle lay between them and their employment. William Knighton, a government official, captured a little of the journey's peril, in 1853:

> The hardships these [Indian] coolies undergo in travelling on foot through the jungles of Southern India and those of North Ceylon are but little known ... They must arrive within a certain limited period in the plantations district for their supply of food is small, or otherwise they would perish in the forests – hence accidents of a comparatively trivial kind are often death to them for their companions cannot wait; the race is for life and they must sacrifice one, or run the risk of all being destroyed. Hence the disabled member of the gang is necessarily abandoned, deep in the recesses of the forests, among wild beasts and serpents.... [His friends] can do no more ... lying helpless at the foot of the tree, he sees them leave a bowl of rice, the little shell of water by his side ... his outstretched arms, his agonizing wails ... fancy the slimy snake, or the wild leopard stealing towards him.

If snakes or leopards or starvation did not get you, then disease might. At the estates, fresh arrivals were usually fatigued from their travel and often ill-dressed and unaccustomed to the mountain chill. Piled then into overpopulated lodgings, labourers were especially susceptible to sicknesses of the gut. Cholera scythed through the population; at times cutting down entire estates' worth of workers in a single sweep. Living conditions were at their worst in the nineteenth century but even in the early decades of the twentieth, the estates workers' mortality rate was roughly three times that of the remaining hill country population.

Treated also with suspicion by Sinhalese – partly due to the immigrants' reputation for ill-health – South Indian women who began to work in the estates once the crop switched from coffee to tea found themselves additionally besieged by the sexual advances of European planters. Few British claims were ever made to offspring that resulted.

It was an exacting existence. There were eighteen-hour work days and limited scope for escape or advancement. All this, in addition to the many daily race-based humiliations of colonialism. Though much of modern Sri Lankan politics is communal clamouring about which group has suffered most in the past 200 years, the smallest voice among these perhaps has the strongest case: it was not until 2003 that all Upcountry Tamils – a group distinct from other Tamil communities on the island – were officially granted Sri Lankan citizenship. Even now, the tea estates continue to function almost solely off their labour.

At first glimpse, the line rooms looked almost pleasant. Low-slung and terraced, with some blocks running the length of three or four cricket pitches, the teal paint on their facades brought to mind the colour of shallow ocean under clear skies. It was only as we descended the hill and drew closer that their imperfections leapt out like a camouflaged regiment springing an ambush. Wind whistled through broken windows and the unpainted side walls betrayed cracked, mud-brick bodies. The roofs of the better homes were of rusted corrugated iron but the shabbier ones were sheltered by black plastic sheets that rubbed and rasped when the breeze blew over them. Pinning these sheets down to the structure was an assortment of detritus: rocks, broken branches, paint cans, and bits of metal so corroded they appeared as though they may crumble at the touch.

We passed groups of chatting women in colourful frocks as we walked in the alleyways between the rows of rooms. They flashed us warm, wide smiles while their children – virtually oblivious to our presence – played with tennis balls on uneven stone paving. Chickens browsed among the gutters. Washing soaked in sooty metal basins outside doorways that had no doors.

With me was Jothipala. He had insisted on coming along, though it was getting late in the day. I had actually discovered on the trishaw ride here that his antipathy toward the colonizing British was couched within a wider loathing of the West. Many of his gripes were coherent. 'Why is it that so many of the Western nations want to point out the problems in our country, when they are the ones starting wars all over the world?' he had asked at one point. Others were pure conspiracy: 'See how much damage these NGOs have done in Sri Lanka, always undermining us. We are a country with good resources no? The *suddha* [white man] just can't stand to see us rise in the world.'

In fact, our relationship had briefly become strained when he learned that in my day job I was employed by a multinational. 'ESPN? What is that? Another NGO?' I had been quick to reassure him it wasn't but his suspicions were unallayed. Only when an old Sinhala song came on the trishaw radio and I seized the chance to ingratiate myself by singing a few lines as casually as I could, did I feel I regained a little of his confidence. Still, perhaps the vibe between us was never fully restored: it is possible he had cast me irredeemably in a new light.

But, having accompanied me this far, Jothipala did keep his promise to introduce me to a friend of his in the line rooms. Coming to a home with chipped outer walls, we met Mr Meiyanathan, a longtime resident of these rooms and a teacher at the local high school.

'Come in, but you'll have to forgive me – I can't offer you any tea,' he said. Mr Meiyanathan was an unsmiling man but his deep wrinkles conferred on him a paternal benevolence. There was an easy warmth about his timbre. 'My children are out, you see, and it'll take a long time to get the water.'

Pointing us to two old cane chairs, Mr Meiyanathan sat down on the edge of a bed in the corner of the double-garage sized family quarters. Six people resided here. In his crisp blue shirt, pressed slacks, and with neatly parted white hair, Mr Meiyanathan himself seemed apart from the clutter around him. To his left, a desk was strewn with plastic plates, photo frames, and a 12-inch TV. Across the room, multicolour threads and fabric cascaded to a coarse cement floor, from a foot-pedal Singer sewing machine. The ceiling was of whitewashed, sewn-together fertilizer sacks.

'We're actually lucky in this estate,' he told us. 'Most of the rooms have electricity and the toilet facilities can normally be maintained decently.' His Sinhala was flecked with a Tamil accent in places but was essentially perfect in substance. 'It can be much worse in other line rooms, I'm telling you. They pack people in like broiler chickens in some places.'

Having been born in the early 1940s, Mr Meiyanathan actually lived on estates run by the last remaining British planters. 'But mostly I just know the stories that my elders told me,' he said.

He spoke haltingly at first, testing the strength of every phrase before committing to it. Only after we had chatted for half an hour did he feel comfortable enough to hold forth on his childhood. He told us about barely seeing his parents through youth, so belaboured were they on the fields. He spoke of growing up feeling he'd never escape estate work, so slim did his prospects seem.

It was the alienation Mr Meiyanathan remembered most of all. He recalled a deep-rooted fear of the planters, and the discomfort he felt in the company of local Sinhalese. Only in the Tamil enclaves on the estates had he felt completely at ease.

'Why were you so anxious around Sinhalese?' I asked.

'That was all intentional – a lot if it was the suddha's doing, over generations.'

'How do you mean?'

The professor in Mr Meiyanathan began to emerge. 'There's one story that has been passed down to me that I'll tell you. Many people don't know this, but on a lot of estates, the British had at least one man patrolling the perimeter of their fields with a gun. Now this man was called an 'appu watcher'. The appu watcher's job, according to the British planters, was to keep the estate safe. But our elders were not quite so gullible. That was not his only job. The appu watcher was also there, in part, to stop us from getting too friendly with the Sinhalayo in the outside village. Whenever someone from a nearby village came to the estate, for example, the appu watcher would spring into action immediately. He'd make his gun very visible, and he'd chase them off. The idea was that we never could establish a connection with the Sinhalayo; we could never conspire together with them.'

But on the plantations, as elsewhere, there had since been little dismantling of the divisions the British had sown. The Sinhalese who began to take over the plantations in the 1950s, '60s and '70s, sought to do business largely in the colonial style, Mr Meiyanathan said. 'What has been the change, you know? Even now, look at how much they pay us.' Two of his three adult children were employed on this estate, which is why he was allowed to live here. The other worked in the Middle East.

'Six hundred rupees a day for the women, is what they give us. Eight hundred only for the men. It is, I suppose, just barely enough to survive on. If you are a man, and the planters like you, you might rise to become a supervisor, or become a manager in the factory. But suppose someone falls sick. Then what? Maybe there is an accident. What to do then? The only thing is to become indebted and that's the thing – that's how they keep you here.'

'You feel trapped?' I asked.

'Well they have put us in a pit, haven't they? Just see the machinery they have at the factories. Half of them are a seventy or even a hundred years old. Just think: how can they run an entire industry like that? The only explanation I can think of, is they keep the labour costs low on purpose. They have kept the British instruments. Just like that, they have also kept us.'

Jothipala had nodded along through much of this and seemed especially sympathetic to Mr Meiyanathan's complaints about the estate's incumbent masters; a colonial axe to grind he did have, perhaps, but he was no myopic Sinhalese nationalist. In fact, when at one stage I had suggested that plenty of upcountry Tamils *had* graduated to the middle class, he quickly made the argument that on almost every economic metric, hill country Tamils were worse off than other races.

'Before, we could blame the suddha,' Mr Meiyanathan said, a little resignedly now. The fire that had briefly taken his voice had fizzled out. 'But now look. The people running the estates and living in the big bungalows while we cram into the rooms here – they are our own, you know; the black white man – the *kalu suddha*.'

In the few days I had been in the hill country, plantation workers were on strike.

In Colombo, strikes and protests had become a regular feature of daily life. Teachers, doctors, veterans, or bus conductors clamoured daylong on the roads for a greater slice of post-war Sri Lanka, creating stationary columns of commuters so irate their blood pressure might launch rockets into outer space.

The estate workers' strike here, meanwhile, was more dignified remonstration than warlike ruction. It was a nuisance only to employers and, even then, labourers took only half-days off, partly because many families could not afford to forego a full day's pay.

When I visited a factory south of Nuwara Eliya in the early afternoon the next day, tea-plucking women were already lining up with their half-empty baskets to have their harvests weighed and graded. I sensed among them a little anxiety; if the foreman deems their takings to be of insufficient volume or substandard quality, they go unpaid for their morning's work. I watched the women file noiselessly into the factory. These were the same sorts of labourers who beamed resplendently in advertisements, wherever Ceylon Tea was sold.

But this was at the rear entrance to the factory. On the other side, next to a modern cafe overlooking an especially ravishing hillside, visitors gathered for guided factory tours. I soon found myself attached to a Chinese group. We were about nine in total. There was one couple with a chubby five-year-old boy, four women probably in their early twenties, the tour guide – a woman named Susanthika – and myself.

I had expected the tour to be an extensive jaunt through the bowels of the factory but on that front it was a severe disappointment. We were taken into a lobby, and merely ushered through a series of viewing stations, where various pieces of machinery could be glimpsed. A withering tray – where the leaves are initially dried – was visible from the first stop. A roller came into view, then a sorter, then a fermenter, and so on. As Mr Meiyanathan had said, the machines were almost always of colonial age.

We were not required to walk more than fifty metres,

so the tour *should* have taken no longer than ten minutes in total, except that our progress was endlessly lengthened, and infinitely enlivened, by my having been with this particular group.

Before the tour had even properly begun, my companions had broken out in mass euphoria when Susanthika produced two fresh tea leaves attached to a bud as an example of what the estate's tea pluckers harvest from the fields. As she passed the leaves around, the factory lobby rang with fevered exclamations of 'Waaaaooow!' Each member of the group also needed at least one photograph with the tea leaves in their palms and, then, when one of the younger women had the idea to pose with the leaves tucked behind her ear, all the other women decided they would just die if they couldn't all be photographed that way – first individually, and then as a foursome, with Susanthika disappearing through a door to fetch more leaves.

Whenever my tour-mates would require a picture with all eight of them (including Susanthika) in the frame, I volunteered to handle the camera, as the group's loner. They insisted on having at least two photos taken at a time. For the first, they would uniformly wear glorious time-of-their-life grins. The moment the first click was heard, they would immediately pull goofy faces, and hold up the 'V' sign. So exact and automatic was this, that I became convinced this must a photographic procedure mandated by the Chinese government.

Towards the end of the tour, Susanthika scooped up a handful of withered, crushed, and rolled leaves from the fermenter and this is when my companions really lost their minds. While the fragrant handful was passed around, the 'waaaaaaaaooooows' rose in pitch, volume, and intensity until every corner of the building pulsed with pure ecstasy. The overhead tube lights glowed brighter; the machinery began to produce sparks. I found myself wishing I loved anything as much as these people loved this handful of tea.

Of the seven tourists, only the little boy showed some restraint. For him were less demonstrative pleasures. When his mother put the handful of the tea in his palm, he looked around, brought it to his face, surreptitiously dipped a tongue into the leaves, then stashed what remained in his pocket. For the rest of the tour, he would periodically dip into his store and smuggle bits of tea into his chubby little mouth, always making sure his parents were not wise to his covert predilection.

As fun as it might have been to spend the remainder of the day in their company, they bade our tour guide and me a touching farewell (by which I mean they had us pose for no fewer than two dozen photographs with them) and piled into the van they had arrived in.

I made my way back to Nuwara Eliya, picked up my things, and left town, feeling a little better than I had the day I'd arrived.

FIVE

Kin and Karma

Much of the next thirty-six hours was a blur of transportation. The first bus ride, to the town of Keppetipola, was interrupted by the vehicle blowing a tyre. Thankfully, the breakdown had occurred in the vicinity of a roadside mechanic and yet, although that should have made it a straightforward tyre change, it required a dozen neighbourhood men to converge on the bus and offer loud and varying opinions before eventually we were in a position to resume the road, almost an hour later.

The second leg of the journey, to Boralanda, was perhaps the noisiest ride of the journey, as working folk going home on the last bus on the route made raucous conversation in all directions. The best of these exchanges was the soaring political diatribe from the two men sitting immediately in front of me. Full of 'out-of-touch, self-serving crooks,' was the government, they concurred. 'What a shame the politicians who care about the *podi miniha* [working man] are not given a proper place.' Except that one was maligning the previous government and the other was trashing the present one, so really they were making opposing points, which perhaps they would have realized had they not both been drunk off their faces.

Arriving then at the tiny central intersection at Boralanda after 9 pm, I press-ganged a young trishaw driver to take me up into the even tinier village of Ohiya. He only agreed after he himself convinced a friend to come along, in case he ran into trouble on the lonely, steep, and wooded nine-kilometre return. 'You never know what will happen up there, no?' he said. 'It gets bloody cold. An animal could come charging out even.'

When eventually I got into the Ohiya guesthouse, I found myself immediately needing to make arrangements for yet another trishaw journey. I had come hoping to visit Horton Plains National Park, which was best viewed just after dawn the following morning, before highland clouds rolled in. The guesthouse owner *had* a vehicle but told me the Russian couple in the adjoining room had booked a ride in it and that I would need to ask them if I could go along. They took some convincing.

AFF: Hi, do you think I can squeeze in with you on the ride to Horton in the morning?

Russian Woman: Sorry, I tink there will not be space in one tuk tuk for all of us.

Russian Man: She is right. We have lot of kamra equipment. You will need odder vehikle.

AFF: I promise I don't take up a lot of space.

Woman: We have bags and dey are very big. We are tinking we will climb two mountains maybe.

Man: Yes, lot of voter bottles. You will need odder vehikle.

AFF: It'll be really tough for me to find something else at this time. You sure all our stuff won't fit in the back near the rear window? It's probably roomier than you think.

Woman: No. It is small tuk tuk. We rode dis today.

Man: Yes, impossible, my friend. You will need...

AFF: OK. I'll pay for the ride.

Woman: You will pay?

AFF: Yeah, I'll take care of the whole thing, both ways.

(Pause)

Woman: Maybe ... ok ... we try to fit in.

Man: Of korse. We make space. No need odder vehikle.

So, I piled in with them at daybreak and, by 7 am, was trekking the beautiful montane *pathana* grasslands of the park, where, at roughly 2200 metres above sea level, conditions are thought to be too harsh for trees to take root. Laced exquisitely by mountain streams and specked by unhurried herds of sambar deer were the wheat-coloured plains, a delicate curtain of mist already beginning to form on their fringes.

Happily unobscured, however, was the view from World's End – the 1000-metre cliff that is the park's primary attraction. There was an oscillating ridge directly opposite the drop, with toy-town houses and lush plantations in the valley between. Towards the poles there were largely unimpeded views: lakes, rivers, and farms to the north, and rolling forests to the south.

The kinds of people who always have to have the best travel stories will say they saw the southern coast from World's End – something I had never previously believed. As I sat on a rock and took in the view, it didn't seem altogether outrageous.

It was at the lookout too, that I had my favourite non-verbal human interaction of the trip. As I ate a vegetable-stuffed roti sitting on this rock, an East Asian couple spotted me and became transfixed, in the way safari-goers might be upon seeing rare wildlife. At first, they viewed and photographed me from a safe distance, wary, perhaps, of sending me scurrying into the bushes. They then inched their way forward, smiling broadly, as if to convey they meant no harm. Each halting advance accompanied by a flutter of camera shutters. Eventually, coming to realize I was quite tame, the man came and sat right next to me while his companion took the pictures. There were a few photos of us sitting side by side, looking together over the drop; a few more with his arm around my shoulder. Finally, the most intimate pose of all: the man turned his back to me, his body at a right-angle to my outstretched legs, and then leant back on his elbows, his back arched over my thighs. Looking hopefully at me, they gestured together that I smile for the camera. When they showed me the resulting snap, the two of us did look gorgeous, with that arresting vista stretching out behind us. We could easily have made the next cover of *Gay Interracial Monthly*.

But it was not a lingering encounter. I soon bade a wordless goodbye to my new friend and his wife, raced out of the park, picked up my bags in Ohiya, and caught the late-morning train out of the village. There was a six-hour descent back west to

Rambukkana – most of it on the same track I had come in to the hill country on. From there, a country bus took me north to the town of Dambadeniya. It was here that, for the first time on the journey, I had arranged to meet my relatives.

Saman *aiya* – older brother in Sinhala – had been waiting for me on the main road with his son, and loading my bag into the back of their Dimo Batta – ostensibly a truck, though it was smaller, end-to-end, than a large sedan – they took me to their home, in the village of Kaudumunna. Once Saman and his wife, Shiromi *akka*, were finished berating the standard of Sri Lankan driving upon hearing about how my forehead got its stitches, they showed me to my room, on the eastern side of their little house.

Next morning, I would proceed to break one of the cardinal rules of provincial living: I slept in past 7 am.

Shiromi, dark, plump, almost forty, and forever bubbling with a joke or a chuckle, was a blood relative, though neither she nor I know exactly how. One theory pegged her as a distant aunt; another suggested we were linked only by marriage. As a general rule, however, it is better not to run too powerful a microscope over Sinhalese family trees. Who knows if successive generations of ancestors will turn out to have been first cousins? Childhood asthma or dodgy joints could do without being cast in such unflattering light.

The point is, exact blood ties were unimportant. Shiromi had been eight when in the mid-eighties, my grandparents adopted her and her younger brother Shiron – their biological mother no longer able to care for them. Half-a-generation younger than my parents, and a little more than a decade older than my sisters and me, they were effectively close, older cousins. Childhood memories of Shiromi come with especial fondness: in our long holiday stints at our grandparents' place, she had taken it upon herself to entertain us kids, often cooking and caring for us as well.

It had been at our grandparents' home, too, that Shiromi and Saman had fallen in love. He, the hard-working carpenter, stole glances as he fitted the new annexe with doors, windows, and cabinets. She, the employers' young ward, made her warm, winning quips when she brought him cups of tea. So plainly thoughtful and good-natured was Saman that it wasn't long before their romance was rubber-stamped by the elders. When they were married, property in Colombo proved beyond their means. They moved here, three hours northeast of the capital, to a village in which they had no family but where otherwise they felt they would lack for little else.

At first look, it was easy to see what had drawn them. Laying within Sri Lanka's coconut-growing triangle, there was barely a view in Kaudumunna from which at least half-a-dozen coconut trees could not be glimpsed. Parrots nested in the village's lush canopies and kingfishers stood watch over little reservoirs. In abundance, also, were rice paddies, banana trees, jackfruit, papaya, mangoes, mangosteens, spiky pineapple tops erupting from the soil, and Buddhism. Hard places, it is said, breed hard people. Kaudumunna locals would not know much about that.

Next morning, in their yard skirted by thambili trees and carpeted by an unsually silky Australian grass, Saman had grown in a tidy rectangular patch, I played cricket with their eleven-year-old son Vaeg. It had been Vaeg, in fact, who woke me up, charging into my room just before eight to announce the match would begin in twenty minutes, so I had better have got dressed and eaten breakfast in time to bowl him the first ball. I would have been annoyed had this not immediately struck me as a sort of generational karma. Once, when I was five, Shiromi's then sixteen-year-old brother had come to our house in Dehiwala to pluck mangoes but learned when he descended the tree that Sri Lankan president Ranasinghe Premadasa had chosen that day to be assassinated and that he would have to spend the next two days of national curfew at our house, more-or-less relentlessly besieged by my demands to play cricket.

Vaeg was a much more accomplished cricketer than I had been at his age and when the match eventually began, only playing my best did I manage to beat him. And amid more matches, and between several cups of Shiromi's sweet tea, a sequence of rural enchantments did that day in Kaudumunna become. Around noon, we picked up a load of timber that Saman would make into a double bed, before he, Vaeg, and I found a flooded quarry to swim in and skipped rocks into the distant granite cliff until our shoulders became sore. The afternoon was spent on the banks of a nearby lake, fishing lines in the water, though nothing was caught apart from bits of lotus stem. Cycling around the village later, as the sun began to set, we bought *aappa* (a crispy, sour rice-flour pancake, known as *appam* Tamil) at a cadjan-hut eatery, decided it would be a shame if we did not eat a few there while they were pan-hot and crispy, and washed it all down with glassfuls of sweet coconut toddy, which had been collected from the tree only moments before.

Fresh air, exercise, a bellyful of good food and drink: so waned the kind of provincial day so idealized in the Sinhalese imagination. Yet, much as I enjoyed Kaudumunna, I was reminded that evening that I was only a passerby. Shiromi and Saman had lived here for thirteen years. For them, not every day was so perfect.

The family had not been invited to the all-night Buddhist *pirith* (blessing) ceremony taking place a few doors down. Still, it was not as if we could not all hear the chanting.

In Sri Lanka, it is generally accepted that if you are a person of faith, your beliefs deserve to be conveyed to all your neighbours, preferably by loudspeaker, and as often and as late into the night as possible. During Easter, for example, many Catholic churches mount speakers on as many telephone poles as it takes for midnight mass to be comfortably heard on the moon. Though no one perhaps matches the Catholics for volume, Buddhist and Hindu places of worship will pride themselves on stamina, broadcasting *bana* – sermons – and religious music for as long as forty-eight straight hours, around special pooja days. Muslims, of course, have the most well-entrenched sleep-deprivation ritual of all – their early morning Azaan. Who knows if this is why jobs in government bureaucracies are pursued so earnestly on the island: in which other profession is there such unhindered access to daytime naps?

In any case, not being invited for this particular all-night pirith ceremony did not sit well with my hosts.

'I told you to go to the temple last weekend, no?' Shiromi clucked at her husband while we tucked into the rest of our aappa and curries, sitting on the newly-built divans in their living room. 'But you didn't listen, did you Saman? Now see what has happened.'

'What's the problem?' I inquired, trying to catch up.

Saman sucked his teeth. 'The people in this village think we are not strong enough as Buddhists.'

'Because we are not – at least not in the Buddhism they are thinking of,' Shiromi said. 'But still, we must go to the temple, no Saman? At least you could have showed your face and come.'

'What happens if you don't go?' I asked.

They looked at each other and chuckled.

'If we don't go ...' Shiromi began, still smirking. 'If we don't go, maybe they will come straight here and shout. They'll go to the temple, chant '*panatipata veramani*' – that they will not harm living things – and then they will march straight here, grab the nearest plank of wood, and beat us.'

Her jests were not without a strain of truth. For all the openness and generosity the majority faith has bestowed on Sri Lankan life, there prevails, in many places, a hard, coercive edge to the manner in which Buddhism is practiced.

Mostly, this takes the form of communal ostracization for non-Buddhists, but if tempers fray to a critical point, violence has been known to spill over.

It seems strange to many outsiders that Buddhism could inspire such fervour in its practitioners. But even the purest, most benevolent ideas are not beyond becoming warped and ugly when welded to exclusionary nationalism. The line of reasoning goes something like this: where Muslims have the Arab world, Christians have the West, and Hindus have India, little old Sri Lanka is the sole home of Sinhala Buddhists and, so, must be zealously guarded as such. Why, hardliners will argue, should Buddhists have to passively bear challenges to their faith, when other religions drive back their enemies with beatings, or bombs, or crusades? Why should Buddhism alone suffer its slights quietly?

And anyway, what in Sri Lanka could possibly deserve preservation more than the island's grand and storied Buddhist tradition? Had Lanka not, after all, been singled out by Lord Buddha as an especially sacred homeland for his teachings? Had Buddhism not thrived under the island's ancient Sinhala rulers, while it waned in India? Had not Lanka's own monks been the religion's foremost evangelists through the middle ages, winning kingdoms in Southeast Asia to the faith? If the temples of Thailand and Laos feel indebted to Sri Lankan Buddhism, what cause could folks such as Shiromi and Saman possibly have to be indifferent to it? You would basically have to be a self-hating Sinhalese, right? That is if you could call a non-Buddhist a proper Sinhalese at all.

Largely lost on most of their neighbours, of course, was the fact that Shiromi and Saman were not actually anti-Buddhist, and that their skepticism was aimed only at the extraneous customs and institutions that had sprung up around the central philosophies of the faith.

'Just see the kinds of things these monks do these days,' Saman complained. 'A few months back, they sent around a group of boys – just teenagers, really – to collect some money. When I asked what the money was for, they said it was to build a wall around the temple. For a wall! As if we don't have people struggling to pay for their medicine in this village.'

For almost a decade, Saman and Shiromi had safely avoided making weekly trips to the local temple but, in recent years, they had begun to feel the pressure to conform a little more keenly. Their standing in the village – which in any case still regarded them as outsiders – had become a little shakier since the arrival of their second child.

Four-year-old Aska was the sweetest, smiling, most affectionate little thing, but a few months into life it had been revealed that she had been born without a corpus callosum, which is the neural bridge that connects the hemispheres of the brain. This slowed her development. Though she now walked and talked, Kaudumunna locals had noticed these milestones arrived later for her than for other children. Blame had to be found somewhere. Unsurprisingly, it settled on the parents. Aska's illness, it was said, was a sort of karmic retribution for Shiromi and Saman's impiety.

For the first time in almost twenty-four hours, my hosts' joyful demeanour gave out, as we talked about their daughter's condition. 'She might have a tough time in life,' Shiromi sighed, feeding Aska her dinner. 'You won't believe what the Montessori teachers said about her.' When they had enrolled Aska in the local nursery earlier in the year, it was soon made clear to Shiromi and Saman that she was not wanted there. 'All sorts of things they were telling us. They told us that children like Aska don't belong in a normal Montessori. "There are enough places to send disabled children like this," they said.'

Saman too, became uncharacteristically subdued and critical. 'See how fake these people's compassion is. When they were telling us she couldn't come back to the Montessori, all the teachers came and ran their fingers through her hair, and said: "*Aney*, how sweet this child is. How sad." If they are really that sad, it would seem to me that they should teach her there. A little extra attention – that's all she needs.'

Thankfully, they had just recently managed to find another Montessori that had agreed to take Aska in – one much further away from home and, being a private institution, a little more expensive. 'It's run by a Muslim teacher,' Saman said. 'Just see – Muslims: the people that us Sinhalese are most suspicious of. When they saw her and we explained to them that she might be a challenge, the lady nicely came and sat with Aska and played with her. I saw that and thought, how much our local teachers could learn by going to visit this place. They need to see how they treat different kinds of children there.'

'Actually, they need to go to this Montessori more than Aska,' Shiromi chuckled.

And, just like that, lightness returned to the conversation. This was what I liked most about Shiromi and Saman. They were no brainless optimists; they took stock of their problems when required. But neither seemed to labour long under the weight of their troubles. Cheerfulness, for them, served a purpose. When life placed an obstacle in their path, it was with humour and wit that they set about whittling it down, until eventually, the problem had lost enough of its initial gravity that they felt themselves able to surmount it.

Through my journey, I would realize this was a trait they shared with many on the island. Perhaps this should not have been a surprise. How else had Sri Lankans borne so gracefully the catastrophes that had heaped themselves, one upon the other, over the past seventy years? Even when people recount their most harrowing days – when they talk about losing everything in the tsunami or of finding their home torched during the 1983 riots, a pithy line or a wisecrack never seems far off. It has been said that Sri Lankans are mirthful despite having had to endure suffering, but I think that is telling it the wrong way around. Maybe it is because of their mirth that so many have endured.

After dinner, Saman withdrew a bottle of arrack from under his bed and the two of us went to their back steps to deplete it by half over the course of a couple of hours. As if in protest, the pirith chanting grew louder and louder.

When, eventually, I went to bed, I was tired and fuzzy-brained. But in a brief, clear-headed moment, I do recall thinking what a conflicted place rural Sri Lanka was. Mostly, it had me besotted. At other times, it infuriated me. I found myself unable, really, to reconcile the two.

SIX

The Primates' Roaring Stand

I had left Shiromi and Saman's the next morning and come to Dambulla. It was for petty reasons that I disliked this town. But the fact remained that I did dislike it.

I will detail my Dambulla grouses only briefly because I may eventually have to return and it would be nice not to be beaten up. Basically: the city centre is a charmless mess, its famous cave temple seems to bestow on the place an excessive sense of self-worth, and – this is the vital bit – several guesthouse owners and restaurant staff have been unnecessarily rude towards me when I've stayed there to cover cricket in the past.

I had only intended to pass through the town on my way further north and, yet, found myself standing for half an hour at a central Dambulla bus halt that morning because the first bus from Dambadeniya had terminated there. Perhaps I have been too harsh on Dambulla because this brief stop went much better than expected. Only twice did I consider throwing myself under the wheels of a passing truck.

Yet, for all its issues, Dambulla does have one great, redeeming feature for the traveller, which is that it is the last urban centre you must pass before Sri Lanka's roads gain their freedom. As roughly two thirds of Sri Lanka's twenty-one-million strong population live in the wet-and-fertile southwest quarter of the island, journeying on the main arteries through those parts is often exceptionally laboursome. If you get far enough from the capital and pass one of the critical waypoints, however – Chilaw on the western coast, Tangalle in the south, or Dambulla, here in the centre – suddenly the sweaty press of civilization gives way to open road; long-awaited relief coming like the undoing of a trouser button after a big lunch.

So when my bus eventually arrived, it positively raced out of Dambulla, left Habarana in the dust, and clattered by Minneriya, familiar woods taking shape outside the window. I had, of course, been through some of these parts when I had begun my journey. But where my initial foray into the dry zone had been brief – an expedition largely to catch the Elephant Gathering while it lasted – I itched to settle in and learn the pulse of the region this time. I had a rough plan of action. I would head first to the medieval ruins of Polonnaruwa before I would double back to the ancient temples of Anuradhapura, hopefully digging up the history of those cities, which are so vital to the Sinhala ethnic identity. Beyond these centres, the Tamil-speaking north – the salt flats of Mannar and the palmyrah-strewn Jaffna peninsula – lay waiting to be touched, travelled, tasted, and understood. After that, the long eastern coast lay in wait. These were the reaches of the island with which I was least familiar and which, it turned out, would deliver the greatest surprises of the journey.

The first cause for astonishment came as the bus approached Polonnaruwa: how extensively the vegetation had been sapped in the three further rainless weeks since I had last been in this vicinity. *Halmilla* trees that had stood hale and stately in September, were now rust-coloured at the tops of their canopies. Rows of teaks, once proud, had seen their broad leaves give in to an undignified droop. Even the creepers – so dogged in normal circumstances – appeared to have shriveled up and given up their advance. The palms alone seemed to bear the oppression with any kind of grace. They listed elegantly as eagles wove lazy circles on thermals above.

In the paddies between the forested stretches, only desiccated shoots and weeds remained – the grain long since having been harvested. Pottering about the fields were farmers wielding torches and cans of kerosene. They systematically set fire to the biological detritus in order to prepare the ground for the next round of tilling and raised columns of grey smoke across the horizon. The smell of burnt grass invaded everything, from the open air, to vehicles, to small-town tea shops – even clothes.

When the bus pulled into Polonnaruwa in the mid-afternoon, I checked into a guesthouse near the ruins and began exploring the town on a hired bicycle in the daylight hours that remained. Here were more signs of fatigue. The old man-made waterways were cracked at the bottom; no more than thin, limping trickles remaining to even the ditches on the lowest ground. The roadsides had been swept nearly empty by the heat. Almost every action seemed to raise clouds of dust.

And yet, not everything had been brought to a halt by the harsh tail end of the dry season. There was life in this town yet. As is ever the case in Polonnaruwa, from up in the canopy came the sound of a little roughhousing.

For all the constrictor snakes, mongooses, monitor lizards, parrots, and football-sized rats that had sometimes made merry in our Dehiwala backyard over the years, I can't recall ever being visited by monkeys. It's not that they are unheard of in Colombo – troupes of langurs are sometimes seen bounding along walls and roofs in the outer suburbs where the city melds with the countryside. But monkeys do not feature in daily life as they do in the inland centres. And nowhere are they as ubiquitous as in Polonnaruwa. Here, hordes of macaques hang off telephone wires, langurs loiter by the dozens near roadside stalls, and bulb-eyed, nocturnal lorises wander around the canopy at geriatric paces. Monkeys are so prolific that the town has been home to the longest-running primate study in the world – now in its forty-fourth year. When I cycled into the research camp the next day, I met Sunil Gunathilaka, one of the lead scientists.

Sunil was a jovial balloon of a man. His cropped, greying beard sprang from full cheeks and he had eyes full of mischief, which as I'd discover later on, lent a warmly comic touch to his every sentence. When first we met, however, he was struggling to keep them open. Once he had introduced himself, led me inside, and sunk himself into a settee, he told me he had been up until three in the morning helping his teenaged daughter with a school assignment, on top of which it was her birthday so he had been cobbling celebrations together, on top also of which he was having to deal with the roofer who was repairing damage that monkeys had caused. 'Can't have holes in the roof when the rain starts, no?' he said. 'My wife has been telling me to get the thing looked after.'

He appeared eager to help when I said I wanted to learn about the study, so at his encouragement, I found myself battering him with questions. What have been the major revelations from this research? How many species lived in Polonnaruwa? Is their habitat being destroyed? Do they steal from the locals? Sunil dutifully fought exhaustion for a few minutes but began to fade in the comfort of his settee. I would be halfway through a question and, slowly, his eyelids would droop. His head would loll back. His mouth would fall open. After thirty seconds in repose, he'd rouse himself with a curt snort, and with a look of mild alarm discover me staring expectantly at him. Once his brain re-engaged he'd reel off an answer. Then the eyelids would descend again.

The air was so close that day even I began to feel an impromptu siesta coming on, but just as my line of questioning was giving out, we were both brought to attention by the agitated arrival of his boss.

Flinty-eyed and direct, Dr Wolfgang Dittus was the longtime director of the study and a much-decorated American primatologist. He struck me the perfect sitcom foil for Sunil as he unsmilingly introduced himself and set about learning who I was and my business at his camp. He wore a faded shirt, a tattered grey cap, beige shorts, and hiking boots. No one could have looked more like a field biologist.

The primate project was his life's work, he eventually told me, taking a seat between Sunil and myself. Having lived in Polonnaruwa since 1968, Dittus had accrued the litany of grievances against the Sri Lankan government that is the prerogative of any long-time resident. The grouses streamed in torrents from him. Three times, Dittus said, he'd been accused of being a CIA spy, until in 1982, he was personally able to convince president J.R. Jayawardene otherwise. With little prompting, he lamented state programmes that saw the expansion of farmland into what used to be forests. A few minutes later, the reputation of the country's Wildlife Department lay in tatters on the research centre floor. 'The thing is, instead of appointing people with any technical knowledge to the wildlife jobs, they get picked by whoever is in power at the time,' Dittus said. 'They just dance to the tune of the politicians.'

It was for the Sri Lankan public that he reserved the most stinging ire. 'These pilgrims who come to Polonnaruwa on big buses – no matter what we tell them – they keep feeding the monkeys.' His speech was even in volume and pitch but there was no mistaking his smouldering rage. 'You know, it's beyond ignorance. It's a stubborn stupidity when they've been told once or twice not to do it.'

The effects of feeding had begun to pose significant challenges to Polonnaruwa's locals because, in many surrounding villages, increasingly fearless monkeys raided shops and homes, taking off with vast quantities of food, causing damage to property in the process. It also proved an obstacle to the primatologists: parts of the monkey population could no longer be considered wild or natural, said Dittus.

He roared on. 'People here have been lied to by politicians for centuries, so they have no regard for authority. When you ask them not to feed the monkeys, just to be polite they will say okay. The moment you turn your back, they've thrown away some food. The only thing they think about is gaining merit for the next life. As soon as they get off the buses, the feeding starts.'

I'm not sure quite how, and it must have been because Dittus was in a particularly foul mood that day, but soon the rant had strayed from primatology and become mired in more worrisome territory.

'The other thing is,' he snapped, 'there is no clue about personal responsibility among these people. It's ... from the time they are born, they expect to have everything given to them. 'Amma will give me, Amma will give me.' Then when they grow older, the government becomes their Amma ... their mother. Everything they expect, they expect it for free.'

Since I am the kind of spineless moron who constantly strains to please new people, I nodded along, earnestly jotting down his pearls of wisdom. This, Dittus must have taken as encouragement.

'You know, you do get the same thing in other countries. In the States you have people living in government housing and living off food stamps – mostly these are Afro-Americans. But here it's something else. Here its more … far more …'

'Widespread?' I completed, before immediately being struck by guilt for having allowed myself to be co-opted in the tirade.

Sunil had sat through the exchange in silence and would only bring himself to respond later that afternoon, when he took me to the old city to track a troupe of langurs. He was spryer company by then. We rode in to the site on his motorbike and met the monkeys in the shade of an adinah tree, which towered above the remains of a medieval Buddhist complex. To our right was a stepped bathing pool, still bearing much of its elaborate stonework; ahead of us a worn, granite staircase led to the craggy remnants of a bhikku's lodging house. When the langurs migrated westward into a *kohomba* grove, we traipsed after them. Sitting in the shade with monkeys foraging around us, Sunil poured forth.

'What Dittus is saying is right, in one sense,' he said. 'But you have to understand that our people have to deal with the monkeys every day. Some will even get so fed up with them that they are willing to poison the monkeys. But see, sometimes the same people will feel sorry if they see an injured animal. They call straight away to tell us. You know, you have to understand that's just the way our people are.'

'And anyway,' he went on, emboldened by my appreciative murmuring at this stirring defense of our people, 'where's the biodiversity in Europe? Their wild primates have all gone extinct apart from a few in Gibraltar. What happened?'

More to the point, in how many places do wildlife

populations come off stronger – at least numerically – for their brushes with humanity? I had expected monkey numbers to have declined over the last few decades but they are, I was told, in the midst of a rambunctious boom that has stretched three decades. Macaques are the sharpest of the four Sri Lankan species and it is their numbers that have spiked most dramatically, having increased by about thirty per cent since the mid 1980s. Locals say macaques will ravage banana orchards on a weekly basis, rummage through trash for edible bits, snatch chocolate bars out of toddlers' fingers, then sneer at the children from the treetops.

'When I came to the study in 1986, there was much less of this trouble,' Sunil said, the langurs now having formed rows to pick ticks off each other's backs. 'But Polonnaruwa has become more sophisticated. There are tube wells everywhere in the village, so the water is even more abundant. And now, with the genetically-engineered crops also, there is access to year-round food.'

There is not much locals can do about this though the authorities, in their wisdom, have of course suggested to them that in addition to covering their food so the flies don't get in, and lighting coils to chase away mosquitoes, and burning the grass to keep snakes at bay, and avoiding night-time travel for fear of wandering elephants, they must also keep their garbage sealed inside the house to discourage macaque raids, as well as build walls around their wells and taps, if they don't mind. So much of rural Sri Lankan life seems to be about beating back this relentless onslaught of the wild.

In fairness to nature, however, humans partly have

themselves to blame for a centuries-long proliferation of wildlife – in this town at least. A few hundred metres from where Sunil and I had sat, just out of sight, lay Polonnaruwa's immense medieval tank. Although it had been diminished a little by five rainless months, the surrounding forest continued to be nourished by the waters that have nurtured it for almost a millennium. In the tank's defiance of the long, dry season, the wild has found its own means of resistance. The vegetation may wilt towards the end of September and the animals may become languid. But ultimately, flora and fauna survive. When the rains return, they thrive.

Unlike most reservoirs in the province, the tank at Polonnaruwa commands national reverence. This is partly thanks to its size but also a reflection of the esteem in which the king who built it is held. Politicians invoke his name in screeching speeches about Sri Lanka's glorious past and the public invokes it to lambast the comparative shortcomings of present rulers. The ancient Dutugemunu may be the conqueror of modern Sinhala fancy, but there is little doubt: Parakramabahu I is the island's favoured governor. To him, most often, goes the prefix 'maha': Parakramabahu the Great.

Like Dutugemunu, he had brought the island under single dominion, but perhaps it is because his foes had been other Sinhala kings that his conquests are not themselves extravagantly mythologized. Invading South Indians are so much easier to vilify – ready antagonists do foreigners with an unfamiliar language and religion make.

Nevertheless, Prakramabahu's triumphs in the twelfth century were impressive. At one time, he was forced to wage battle on two fronts: against a ruler named Gajabahu in the north and the tenacious Manabharana in the south. As much as anything, it was the political skill for which he would later be renowned that saw Parakramabahu prevail. Binding together a coalition of old Sinhala clans (uneasy allies themselves), companies of Tamils, and indigenous Veddhas, he disposed of Gajabahu first and, after a back-and-forth struggle, crushed the Manabharana army on the banks of the Mahaweli river. Upon Parakramabahu's capture of Polonnaruwa – by then the island's seat of power for over a century – a tenuous peace took hold.

It was 1153. The wars for the crown had run for five years; the prosperity that descended, for thirty-three.

Partly due to a regional increase in commerce, trade boomed as never before. The brickwork foundations of the medieval bazaars still line the roads of the ruined old city and, in their time, would have been frothing with merchants: Arabs selling silver and perfume, Cambodians and Siamese flogging dyes and spices, Chinese tenderly running their fingers over bolts of imperial silk. From the ports of Mannar and Gokanna (now Trincomalee), Sri Lankan gems and grain were carried off across oceans and the proceeds funneled towards immense construction projects. Of these, none was more ambitious than Parakramabahu's joining together of several lakes into one vast *samudraya*, or sea. With much admiration do Sri Lankans repeat a mantra attributed to the king: 'Let not a drop of rain water go to the ocean, without first benefiting man.'

The reservoir sits now a brooding denim blue under clear skies, with cranes skimming the surface, and elephants coming to drink along its serrated western edge. The eastern bank borders the town and children play in the shallows in the evening. Fishermen paddle out in slim *oru* canoes piled with basket nets.

No infrastructure project – ancient or modern – is more beloved on the island and yet, until earlier this decade, archaeologists had been grossly ignorant of the Samudraya's original size. They had thought it merely Sri Lanka's salient medieval achievement, when perhaps it was the greatest man-made body of water on the planet in its time.

But it was no crack team of experts who discovered this. It had taken a rank outsider from the working class, with no serious academic training, to set the record straight.

During our afternoon watching monkeys together, it had been Sunil who passed on Indika Manawadu's number and urged me repeatedly to get in touch. 'This boy has a great story, ah,' he had said, his mongoose eyes aglimmer. 'What he has found is incredible. Hasn't got enough credit for it also.'

I met Manawadu the next day and understood why national renown may have evaded him. He was a serious man with a moon face and angular eyebrows. Although perceptive and possessed of a brooding intelligence, he had all the charisma of a coconut husk.

We had met at a restaurant, but he said he had already eaten, so he watched me wolf down my rice and curry while I teased out details of his discovery in between mouthfuls. Reticent at first, he eventually began to stitch the tale together. It was a good one.

In 1998, Manawadu had been selling ice-cream from a modified trishaw, not long after graduating high school. One day, parked a few kilometres from the Polonnaruwa town, he noticed a seven-foot bank of earth running through the length of an open field. It intrigued him briefly but he initially thought little of it: deposits of soil dug up in the building of a pond, perhaps, or old mud dredged up from the lake. But as he roamed the area in his trishaw over the following months, he began to see similar earthen protrusions in fields and woods further north. There was an embankment running across a waterway near the village of Lakshauyana; another skirted paddies nearby.

Eventually it occurred to him that they might be old bunds – the levees that bounded the man-made lakes. Out of nothing more than personal curiosity, he began to investigate.

Often thrashing through forests and giving up more than a few pairs of shoes to the mud, Manawadu followed these banks on foot and soon made the discovery that had eluded Sri Lankan and British archaeologists for centuries. The banks were not remnants of several small lakes, as he initially thought. They were what was left of a single, extensive bund. What's more, at its southern edge, it appeared to have once connected with the present levee of the Parakrama Samudraya.

The implications were immense. The Samudraya's bund, he found, had stretched for more than twice its present distance of 12.5 kilometres. With the aid of maps and land surveying data, he estimated the reservoir itself to have covered an area three times its extant 2,100 hectares. For the first time, it began to become clear why Parakramabahu's work was singularly named a samudraya when the island's other reservoirs had uniformly been *wew* or lakes.

Unsurprisingly, the academic establishment was initially reluctant to take Manawadu seriously. They had ignored his advances for years, palming him off as a well-meaning but misguided rural nutjob until, by chance, Manawadu met a local popstar by the name of Dharshana Ruwan Dissanayake in 2009. Initially skeptical, Dissanayake was persuaded to visit the bund sites Manawadu had discovered. He became so convinced of the theory's veracity that he took time out of his own schedule to popularize the findings. Drumming up support from the media, he generally lent Manawadu's enterprise the appeal it had previously lacked.

Eventually the Archaeology Department was prevailed upon to grant Manawadu a proper audience and there he produced for them the evidence he had unearthed over years: well-preserved samples of 800-year-old cistern sluices, washed out stone inscriptions that he had translated himself, as well as half-buried granite marking posts along the length of this newly-discovered bund.

It did not take the establishment long to accept the findings. They had Manawadu produce a paper on the discovery and sent their own staff out to inspect and verify the sites. One professor was so enamoured of the work that when Manawadu's paper was published in the 2013 journal, he slipped his own byline into the article and hijacked half the credit.

After lunch, Manawadu took me on his motorbike to his house. He has not had to sell ice cream for many years but neither has his work landed him any great wealth. We spoke in a cluttered front room with cream coloured walls and a small TV playing cartoons, while his toddler flitted about the legs of a wooden dining table.

'The Archaeology department has actually asked me to come and work for them, but I don't want to do that because if I go there, I will also be in their academic bubble, no?' he reasoned. 'Maybe I won't see things from my perspective.' He told me he was working on another potentially important theory: that the reservoir's waters had in fact surrounded Parakramabahu's palace, making an island out of the royal complex. 'But I need more proof,' he said. 'I don't expect the theory to be accepted easily – the evidence must be there.'

I left Manawadu that afternoon and visited a local doctor to have the stitches taken out of my forehead. The cut had not bothered me much since the evening of the accident, but the unsightly black sutures had brought two infants to tears on the bus ride into town. Between the wound and my birthmark, I also looked like someone who had just been attacked, and maybe defecated on, by a crow. The doctor, thankfully, appeared more impressed than repulsed.

'Ah, there's a good scar' he smiled as his tweezers drew the thread from under my skin. 'Better to come up with a good story for it, isn't it? Say you were defending a girl in a fight.'

I decided I liked him, as I lay on the bed in his small office. I already knew I liked this town. Polonnaruwa seemed to me a place of small wonders; a place of magnetic and manageable chaos, where tenacious macaques make a roaring stand against the bigger, smarter, human primates, and where banks of dirt make archaeologists out of ice-cream salesmen. The ruins and lake may beckon the visitor to the town but in the air there is a whispered promise that if you stay, and you study, and you look hard enough, Polonnaruwa will reveal to you its treasures – it will peel its layers back and pull you into its hidden delights.

But I also knew that I could never live in Polonnaruwa and I would be remiss to leave you unacquainted with the town's more sinister aspect. It pains me to say that nowhere else was I made to feel so unwelcome by a subset of the local population. No place else was I the subject of such visceral and unrelenting hostility.

The problem had begun on my first evening in town. Cycling back to the guesthouse in the dark, I had startled a dog sleeping on the edge of the road. Though my bicycle had not even come close to making contact, the dog emitted a furious yelp and began to give chase. Within seconds it had convinced all its friends in the neighbourhood that I had been out to do it ill. At least half a dozen dogs joined the pursuit, nipping at my back tyre and pedalling legs, growling, teeth bared, and ears pricked.

Vicious, snarling locals – the pack escorts the author to his lodgings.

I returned to my room unbitten on that occasion but tensions failed to abate overnight. The dogs of Polonnaruwa had seemingly decided I was an unqualified threat. Wherever I rode through town over the next forty-eight hours, they came at me from all directions. They bounded over fences, darted out from beneath parked trucks, and ambushed me in packs when I rounded corners. Some even left meals half-eaten and pups untended to make their charge, such was the intensity of their hatred.

Soon there were so many baying in my wake, I was convinced animals must have been recruited from neighbouring towns to this righteous war. At least three dogs would chase me at a time and, when they grew tired, a few more from further down the road would enter the pursuit. I was more or less perpetually passing through a gauntlet of exposed fangs and flying saliva.

What was worse is that though I was often in visible distress, not one person would do a thing to help. I would be riding through town with this savage canine escort and folks would merely look on bemused as if this was some planned city parade, before going back to scratching their genitals, or daydreaming about making out with their sister, or whatever these morons were doing.

Towards the end of my time in town, the dogs even began to make sudden lunges at the bicycle, putting me in danger of swerving into an oncoming lorry, or wrapping myself around a telephone pole – events that, I am sure, would have sent the pack into mass euphoria. I generally wish no harm upon mammals I do not personally find delicious but, on my last evening, I decided that nothing would please me more than to see a few Korean restaurants open their doors here.

But although dogs had filled me with fear on my nighttime jaunts, it was perhaps elephants that I should have been more wary of. On the morning of my departure the owner of my guesthouse told me a woman had been knocked into a ditch by a wandering elephant the previous evening, not far from town. Like a mudslide collecting sediment on its path down the hill, the tale grew more dramatic as the hours went by. I was initially told the woman would had only been a little shaken up, but a three-wheel driver swore she still lay unconscious in hospital. Later on, two women at the bus stand wondered if she would ever walk again, as one of her legs had been crushed. It was past midday when the bus to Anuradhapura pulled out of town and began to motor west. By that stage, the town had not quite got around to killing her yet.

SEVEN

Bloom, Decay, Rebirth

It is an observable fact that even the most cynical people are thrilled when outsiders speak well of their nation. New Zealanders will break into broad grins when they hear about the friendliness of their citizens; Britons will sit up and nod vigorously at appreciations of the nation's laws and order; South African eyes will twinkle at glowing reports about their wildlife; Nepalis who have never been up into the hills will practically hug any traveller that broaches the majesty of their Himalayas. Even in the truly embattled states, where insects are the staple food, and most people have been personally beaten up by the prime minister, hearts probably swell when foreigners shower compliments upon their land.

This is a condition that afflicts Sri Lankans more than most because for decades the only knowledge many outsiders had of the island was that it was home to a brutal civil war. Now, as Sri Lanka tops global must-visit lists and millions descend on the nation, Sri Lankans have gained access to the kind of gushing foreign praise they have long yearned for. It is one of the great feel-good developments of the post-war years.

So who could possibly blame me when, on the first of my two evenings in Anuradhapura, I put down my book and began to eavesdrop intently on two young European women lavishing accolades on my motherland in the verandah of our guesthouse?

'Zees is such an interesting place, no?' one excited Frenchwoman exclaimed. 'I sink I 'ave never been to a country that people are so 'elpful as 'ear.'

'Oh yah, and de food is super,' her German companion offered. 'I hed uhh... kotter roti dis evening vith dis spicy sort of soss. It vos so testy.'

They went on apace, dwelling fawningly on the serenity of the hill country, the beauty of the beaches, and the lustre of Sri Lankan smiles. As I sat bathing silently in all the plaudits, my eyes grew damp and a lump formed in my throat. Such was the welling of pride when they began to laud the marvels of Anuradhapura's ancient Buddhist monasteries, I began to feel as if I had laid the bricks on those 2000-year-old stupas myself.

Eventually, I couldn't help but add my personal spin on this Lanka love-in. I introduced myself and was soon relaying to them the joys of the rice-flour aappa ('I'm telling you, they are even tastier than kottu roti'). I talked up Nuwara Eliya tea ('One good cup, hot and golden, and you'll never drink anything else'). I raved about the leopards at Yala National Park ('Seeing a predator like that in the flesh ... you know ... it changes your life').

Talk of wildlife led easily to the subject of strays and soon they began pulling up photographs of 'cute' dogs they had come across on roadsides. When the Frenchwoman showed me one she particularly liked, my first thought was that it looked exactly like the flea-ridden piece of work that strews garbage across our Dehiwala road and defecates on our front steps. But as national reputation was on the line, I forced myself to behold it smilingly and mustered affectionate noises. The German thought the dogs looked healthy for stray animals. 'Do dey get some kind of professional heltcare?'

'Well, most of them do,' I lied.

In my defence, this kind of embellishing of the nation's virtues is a storied Sri Lankan tradition. Even way back in the first century, four island envoys to Rome had led ancient chronicler Pliny the Elder to believe that Anuradhapura's rulers were 'chosen by the people' and had to be an 'aged man always, distinguished for his mild and clement disposition'. In fact, it was not until the twentieth century that any meaningful form of democracy came to Sri Lanka. Very few leaders have been 'mild' or 'clement' in any case.

Having fawned sufficiently over the dogs, I had moved on to acclaiming the joys of arrack to the women, when an unfortunate thing happened. A sweaty Austrian – face flushed, and hair matted – flopped into the verandah and brusquely introduced himself. Bearded and seemingly in his mid-thirties, he said he was an ardent follower of Buddhism. Quickly it became clear it was to the sound of his own voice that he was most devoted. Upon hearing our adulation for Sri Lanka, a putrid counter-narrative did he spout.

'Actually Sri Lanka hasn't really been dat good for me,'

he snapped. 'I came here thinking dere vud be real Buddhism here, you understand? I vent to Thailand and I vent to Bali and I vos disappointed about their Buddhisms. I thought I vud find it here because Sri Lanka took Buddhism to some of dose countries. But dis is not Buddhism. It's shit. Dat Buddhism is already gone. I am already too late.'

He rattled off a sweltering explanation.

'Der Buddhists here, dey all say dey don't eat meat, but dey do man. Dey are killing chickens and fishes every day. Deir poor fucking elephants are also being kept in deir temples. Dis is not animal velfare. It's shit.'

He went on like this for several minutes, impugning Sri Lanka's littering culture and slandering the nation's lack of driving etiquette, spittle flying copiously from his mouth and the vein on his forehead in a state of violent spasm. The women bore his rants politely, occasionally interjecting to suggest that surely things were not as bad as he was making out. I, however, found myself stricken dumb by a rising anger. At one point he complained that the heat was too much for him. Then, apparently, Sri Lankan bars were trying too hard to be Western. Even the water out of the nation's taps tasted 'like kemikals' to this guy. I mean, for fuck's sake.

There was only so much of this I could take so, I got up, mumbled a goodbye, and headed back to my room.

But seriously, what a prick. Only Sri Lankans should ever be allowed to trash this country to anywhere near that extent.

Lying as it does on Asia's major maritime route, the island has always attracted tourists and drawn their judgement, whether locals have liked it or not.

Ibn Battuta and Marco Polo – the great travellers of their age – had both made landfall here. While Polo's account dwells on Sri Lanka's precious stones and Mongol emperor Kublai Khan's unsuccessful attempts to acquire the 'grandest ruby that ever was seen' from a Lankan king, Battuta, the more priggish of the two, left a more extensive description, writing first of his disdain for the northern monarch who received him and, later, a little more appreciatively of his trek to the summit of Adam's Peak.

But each of those reports come to us from the latter half of the middle ages, centuries after Sri Lanka's longest-serving capital had entered its decline. To find an account that brings to life the mellow grandeur of ancient Anuradhapura, we must look further back in time, to the fifth-century chronicle of the Chinese monk Fa-Hien.

Fa-Hien's journey certainly had been epic. In a seventeen-year expedition, he braved the forbidding Gobi and Taklamakan deserts, rounded the Himalayas, crossed the Indus valley, and, later on, was diverted by a great squall to the island of Java. And yet, he was not your typical rough-and-ready adventurer. Born in 339 CE, Fa-Hien was sixty when, finding the store of scriptures in China 'mutilated and imperfect', he resolved to retrieve from Buddhist lands the religious texts that might strengthen monastic life at home, in Ch'ang-gan.

By the time he arrived in Sri Lanka via Nepal and India, he found his library greatly swelled but his original company thinned. His friends, he writes, had been 'separated from him, some by death, and others flowing off in different directions'. So homesick did he become in Sri Lanka that at one stage he reports being brought to tears by the mere sight of silk.

Nevertheless, he spent at least two years on the island, copying and translating various manuscripts, and making more religious sketches. Much of his time he passed in the great monasteries of Anuradhapura. The then-flourishing temple complex of Abhayagiri he describes with particular relish:

> There is in [Abhayagiri] a hall adorned with carved and inlaid work of gold and silver ... in which there is an image of Buddha in green jade, more than twenty cubits in height, glittering all over ... and having an appearance of solemn dignity which words cannot express.

More striking than the visual description are the numbers that Fa-Hien so casually throws out. Abhayagiri, he says, was home to no fewer than 5,000 bhikkus. South of this, another temple complex hosted 3,000 bhikkus. East of the city, probably at Mihintale, another 2,000 monks resided. Even for the present day, these are remarkable figures – no modern monastery anywhere in the world accommodates more than 1000 monks. For the early fifth century, when the island's total population was no more than a few hundred thousand, they are stunning.

So, when I went to the ruins at Abhayagiri the next day, I tried to picture the ancient saffron-clad multitudes going about their daily lives. Around me, in all directions, lay ragged rectangles of brick and stone – the bases of what had once been wooden libraries, meeting halls, and lodgings. Did they, as centuries of Sri Lankan art suggested, go in dignified columns at dawn, to the terraced bathing pools on the lower levels? Did they line the edges of the hollowed-out stone table, with wooden bowls in hand, to scoop up their daily meal? Did they gather to discuss news from the royal palace in the curious little alleyways?

For the rest of the day, with Fa-Hien as my guide, I trekked and cycled around the vast old city, bigger by several orders of magnitude than Polonnaruwa had been. I came upon innumerable little stupas, once so carefully crafted, now crumbling, half-sunk, and having acquired skins of vegetation, yet all the more beautiful for embodying the process of decay and material impermanence which are such central tenets of the faith. I circled the larger and better-tended stupas of Jetavanaramaya and Lankaramaya, which along with Abhayagiri, had been lost to the jungle for about 800 years following the fall of the Anuradhapura kingdom. Exhumed in the nineteenth century, they have undergone a reincarnation of sorts.

Of these major stupas the most spectacular rebirth belonged to Ruwanwelisaya. It stood lustrous, white, and golden-tipped in the centre of the sacred city, taller than any other monument on the island at 103 metres. Like the other stupas, Ruwanwelisaya had been rescued from the jungle's ravages in the early twentieth century but it was partly because it had had originally been the work of King Dutugemunu – the popular Sinhala conqueror – that it had been resurrected with especial care.

But it was not the stupas that intrigued me most during my day in the sacred city. A few hundred metres south of Ruwanwelisaya rose a vital article of Sri Lanka's Buddhist faith, one both ancient and still living, which at once had lay witness to Anuradhapura's golden age, and yet continued to nourish its believers, along with their hopes and dreams for the future.

Sometime around 500 BC, Siddhartha Gauthama, a prince from the Shakya clan of northern India, meditated beneath a bodhi tree in Bihar for forty-nine days, attained enlightenment, and became the Buddha, or so tradition would claim.

How a sapling of that bodhi came to Sri Lanka is a matter of mild dispute. The orthodox view holds that Sanghamitra, daughter of the great Indian emperor Ashoka, had cut its southern branch and borne it across the ocean. Others claim it more likely that a Sri Lankan king ordered a cutting be brought to his capital.

What is generally agreed on, however, is that having prospered in Anuradhapura's soil since roughly 236 BC, the Jaya Sri Maha Bodhi is the most ancient human-planted tree on the planet. To put its age in context, the tree is older by several centuries than the Roman Colosseum, and only about a decade younger than the Lighthouse of Alexandria, of which, of course, nothing now remains.

This is the thing about Anuradhapura. The casual tourist might become jaded by its vastness or its endless carousel of temple sites but the moment you begin to contemplate the scale of the city's history, you find yourself blown away.

I was particularly astonished to work out while I visited the Jaya Sri Maha Bodhi in the afternoon that when Fa-Hien wrote about the tree 1,600 years ago, it was then already around 650 years old – it's planting as distant from him, as the Bubonic plague was from me. He had written too, about the tree's remarkably ambitious spread. Rising up from behind a protective wall and gilt fence, its branches diverged – unusually for a bodhi – from the lowest part of the tree, like many fingers from an outstretched palm rather than out of a thick singular trunk. This particular shape helped bring as much of the Bodhi's surroundings under its canopy as the strength of its branches allowed. Supporting this expansion were man-made, metal poles, which, painted in gold and decorated, propped up the weaker branches. The tree had had this kind of assistance since at least the fifth century.

'As the [Jaya Sri Maha Bodhi] bent on one side towards the south-east, the king, fearing it would fall, propped it with a post eight or nine spans round,' Fa-Hien writes. 'The tree began to grow at the very heart of the prop where it met the trunk; a shoot pierced through the post and went down to the ground, where it entered and formed roots that rose to the surface ...'

Around the central tree now, many younger bodhis have been planted so that the entire temple courtyard lays in shade. It was a mid-week day – a scorcher – but multitudes of pilgrims had nevertheless made the trip. They were mostly old women, all clad in white. Some sat cross-legged facing the tree, palms upturned on their knees, in meditation. Others chanted pirith from dog-eared books. Still more lay down flowers and lit oil lamps at the various statues of the Buddha along the periphery of the wall.

It was the coloured prayer flags adorning the Bodhi's protective wall, that revealed most about the tree's hallowed place in Sri Lankan Buddhism. These were mostly made of paper, written on and hung up by the pilgrims. 'May the Sri Maha Bodhi bless my daughter Irushi with a child,' read one, in Sinhala. 'May Indrajith be bestowed with the wisdom to pass his scholarship exam,' said another. Others, many very specific, entreated the Bodhi for resources to build a house, for relief from kidney disease, for a visa to work overseas, for favour from an employer.

After I had sat in the courtyard for half an hour, a dark, spindly woman, white hair streaming from her temples into a bun, caught my attention. She wanted help hanging up the string of yellow flags she had made on behalf of her son. He had been married three years, with no children as yet.

'Where have you come from?' I asked.

'From Kalutara. We left early morning.'

'There's a sacred temple in Kalutara itself, isn't there? You came all this way?'

She smiled. 'You must not be a Buddhist. What religion are you?'

I stalled, failing to find the words to quickly explain my convoluted theological position, which in any case I have enough trouble explaining to myself.

'Christian?' she ventured.

'Sure, let's go with that.'

'Well, in your religion you have Jesus, whom you can ask for things you lack, no? In Buddhism we don't have that. The Buddha was a teacher.'

'So, you come here?'

'The Buddha was blessed with enlightenment under this tree. Maybe it has blessings for us also.'

When we had hung her flags up from the gold fence, she returned to sit with the group of women she travelled with, all in spotless white blouses and skirts. They chanted away the afternoon, occasionally breaking into a verse of *gaatha* or *bhakthi gee* – Buddhist hymns.

I would leave Anuradhapura the next day and cross over into lands belonging to a different religion, where another language was spoken. But I would come across this scene again. There too, old women huddled together on sacred ground and prayed for success, fertility, and healing, much of it on behalf of their children.

EIGHT

An Outpost

On the bus ride to the northwestern coast, a roadside statue of a saint brought her to mind again. Though my grandmother was Tamil by ethnicity, she spoke each of Sri Lanka's major languages with aplomb and never really made a big deal about race. Her religion, however, she held very dear.

When we stayed with her during the school holidays, I would find her reciting the rosary on the front steps each morning, an immaculately-tended Bible and a Catholic monthly open on her lap. Under no circumstances was this ritual ever to be disrupted. Once or twice, I had been impertinent enough to make inquiries about breakfast. On such occasions, her lips had continued their dash through the rosary words, but such was the ire in her eyes, they sent me pelting back into the house, stricken with dread.

In the evenings there was a second course of devotions: refrains of 'Hail Mary' or 'Glory Be' whispered over the commercial breaks of her favourite teledramas. But these were only the fainter expression of her piety; more dramatic demonstrations would come when an on-screen couple became even mildly intimate. The moment a brazen embrace or a shameful holding of hands was glimpsed, my grandmother was all scandalized fury, sucking her teeth, scrunching up her nose, spitting a scornful 'chhee!' at the screen, squinting in disgust.

Not that she ever stopped watching, though. The public show was enough.

It had been during the commercial break in one of her shows that, much later in life, my grandmother took the extraordinary step of interrupting herself mid-incantation. I recall being staggered – not only had our trespasses gone unforgiven as per Lord's Prayer, but a grave look had also descended. Fingers still curled tightly around her rosary, she propped her elbows on the arms of her chair and fixed her eyes on me. Her tone was firm. 'What is this I hear from your mother about you wanting to become a journalist?' I had only begun to dabble at that stage, but this was enough to worry her. 'What for? You know, don't you, how very dangerous a job being a journalist is? People are being murdered all over. Yes, so what if it's needed? Why you? Why not someone else? There are other jobs.'

Though placated eventually by the thought that no one had yet been killed for reporting on cricket, my grandmother did, nevertheless, have a point. For so much of her life, which had been lived either in actual wartime or in the long, heated approach to the conflict, good Sri Lankan journalism had been relentlessly besieged. Generations of politicians had shouted reporters down in press conferences and shamed them from campaign podiums. Ministers had had their goons make chilling phone calls and menacing visits to family homes. These were distorted times, for a nation-at-arms prefers propaganda to truth – its war aims spurred by one, eroded by the other. One high-ranking government minister once told a friend of his method of dealing with troublesome journalists: 'First, I will talk to the bugger. If that doesn't work, I will buy the bugger. If that doesn't work, I will whack the bugger.' (The word 'whack' borrowed here from the lexicon of the American mafia.)

The result was nationwide proliferation of misinformation. Uncomfortable facts were shot at, shelled, then smelted and remoulded by the state's media manipulation machine. Half-truths and fabrications were, in turn, lapped up by a southern population whose primal desire for self-preservation aligned perfectly with the government's. Warped was the Sri Lanka of my childhood: Tamils had barely been discriminated against, the northern people eagerly awaited liberation from the LTTE, and Sri Lanka's forces were intractably, unflinchingly heroic. Alternative narratives were scoffed at. To disagree was to betray.

In the years that closely followed the war's conclusion, press freedoms were trod upon evermore while the government railed against grave war-crimes allegations. One newspaper editor was gunned down in his car; others were forced to flee the country. Soon enough, the press was almost uniformly self-censoring, venturing only the mildest critiques, veering clear of prickly subjects entirely. While Sri Lankan journalism was clasped in manacles, the foreign press provided little succour, dealing liberally in fire-and-blood cliches about the north and largely failing to grasp the complexities of this conflict. The truth lay wherever you put your faith. No version of events was without error.

As the bus passed that statue and crossed into the northern province, I thought about all the falsehoods I must have absorbed about the region in which the war had been fought. I wondered how many oversimplifications had shaped my view of the people here; the misconceptions I must still hold about their towns. It occurred to me that this was the band of the island I had read the most about, and yet, understood the least. I resolved to emerge from these travels less of a stranger to these parts. I resolved to listen closely, to see for myself, to take on board the stories, and shed the deceits.

Outside the bus window, it was as if a curtain had parted. As we tracked toward the coast on recently-rebuilt roads, gone were the heartland's bodhi trees and Buddhist temples. Gone were the lake beds with their mud-bathed water buffalo. Hardier livestock wandered here: goats and chickens. Instead of forests, here was scrubland. Instead of paddy fields: salt flats. Settlements were sparse, Tamil script dominated the shop hoardings, and the air smelled of dust.

There were also fewer folks in these parts. Even for a Saturday, the roads appeared deserted. Life here seemed to travel at a different pace.

If being an island makes Sri Lanka laidback, it may explain why Mannar – a smaller island off the northwest shoulder – is laidback squared. When I arrived via the bridge from the mainland late that afternoon, Mannar's major town, which goes by the same name, was already easygoing enough. Traffic cops leant idly against store fronts and street vendors stirred only to languidly slap their own faces, the flies they were attempting to deter themselves moving in slow motion.

On Sunday, the town was evermore suspended. On near-silent roads bicycle wheels spun with droll reluctance; in near-empty restaurants an age passed before new customers became noticed by staff.

Interspersed with this indolence were snatches of island verve. The Urban Council's hot-pink paintjob and entranceway adorned by streamers made it appear more a wedding reception hall than the town's bureaucratic hub. Intersections, meanwhile, were guarded by Mannar's bright plaster saints; lanes were presided over by kingfisher-blue arches topped with dazzling crosses.

It was the droves of wandering donkeys that tried hardest to bring the place to life. They are a vestige of the town's medieval glory days, when, as Sri Lanka's major port, Mannar drew traders from all over Asia and North Africa. Once perfumes and textiles arrived here, the donkeys had borne goods to the inland kingdoms and carried Sri Lanka's own produce out again.

Though they have traipsed around Mannar since the ninth century, the donkeys' plight has recently grown grim. When the war hit, some of their owners skipped town. Many of those that remained could not afford to care for their animals. Let loose over the last few decades, the donkeys have now acquired a feral streak, roaming Mannar's streets, in hee-hawing, dung-strewing packs – pests, when even within living memory, they had been instrumental to the livelihoods of so many.

They are especially fond of chasing each other, locals say, often into fences, telephone poles, ditches, or small children. One story has a fleeing donkey leaping straight into a passing trishaw and emerging clean out the other side. Another has a passed-out town drunk being repeatedly tracked down and urinated on by the same animal, night after night.

When a female is in heat, her spirit is said to reach an unbearable zenith. Males flock from all around the town, their famously hefty instruments engorged, a trail of obscenely erect suitors collecting in a queue. Nightlong braying, head butting, and jockeying for position ensues and, next day, Mannar parents are posed uncomfortable questions by their children, outside whose windows the randy parade had come to its debauched conclusion.

An endearing oddity did Mannar seem at first. Its present had given into lethargy. Strains of its past were attempting to shake the place awake. The colours were manic, the people were mellow; everything threw everything else into relief.

The morning after I arrived in town, I met Elijah Hoole. I had previously only encountered him online through his articles on race and post-war politics. He wore a faded polo and a blank expression when we met but, beneath this Mannar uniform, a fierce wit lurked. His writing in English was persuasive enough but, at twenty-four, he had written for Tamil national dailies as well. Lately, final-year work for his engineering degree had him occupied. He pinballed from coast to coast, splitting time between an internship in Colombo, university in the east, and home, here on this island off the island.

'Two questions people will ask, when you say you're from Mannar,' he told me at breakfast. 'The first is whether you drink. The second: whether you play football.' Of football I had seen little evidence the previous day but there seemed no shortage of the alcohol-addled after the sun had set. 'It's that *machan* culture of just getting together with your friends. But then it is a small place also. If you go somewhere for a drink, before you even open the beer your family will know.'

It is easy to forgive Mannar this vice, because how else to bear the particular horrors that fighting lavished on the region? During the war years, the island was cut off – the land and rail bridges having been bombed into disuse. The only way out was by sea. Trips to the mainland, Elijah said, were 'like going abroad'.

He recalled the hardships his family had faced on their annual trip to the capital. 'The vomit swirling on the boat deck' remains crystallized in his memory, as do the cramped conditions and always having to embark in the night due to various security threats. 'The thing I really remember though, is the smell of the place we stayed at overnight. We would get off at Kalpitiya and wait till morning, but there were so many people. It was horrible.'

The remaining distance could be travelled by road and once on Planet Colombo – light years removed from their island – the family would visit relatives and stock up on clothes, medications, sweets, books, bed sheets, kerosene lamps – anything that might be in short supply at home over the coming year. When they returned, many purchases already confiscated by the military, their days were replete with endless home searches and the nights rang with distant artillery fire. 'But the only time we came close to any fighting, was when an army officer was shot by a guy on a motorbike near our house,' Elijah said. 'That was it.'

It was a pity that he retold all this with such scientific dispassion because, to me, his are the kinds of childhood stories that could be endlessly milked for sympathy.

Northerners are, in general, unreasonably understated about the kinds of chilling experiences that would drive most people to quivering nightmares and involuntary urination. Many in these parts have lived through shelling. Some have been threatened at gunpoint or had friends and family members go missing. Others have come face-to-face with violent death. Yet they will recount these ordeals with disarming composure, like they are informing you that mangoes have gone up in price, or that your zipper is down.

In the south, many did, of course, lose life and limb, but the majority did not and yet, upper-class Colombo was a morass of wartime sob stories. The capital was, at times, the outward face of the conflict. When foreigners – from the West, especially – sought accounts of wartime hardship, readily did Colombo step into the breach.

Expectations were even greater for Sri Lankans living overseas, and during my years in New Zealand, I must admit I sometimes found myself pulling on my best I've-seen-some-shit expression and delving into a war-story monologue. I would recall for my friends the agony of being regularly asked for identification at checkpoints, though this usually only affected my parents. My voice would waiver when I spoke of the bomb threats that closed schools down for weeks, despite having been overjoyed at the impromptu holidays. When a well-meaning white person had placed a consoling arm around my shoulder, a distant stare had been assumed, long pauses had begun to punctuate my speech, and a groove had been settled into. What else was I to do, really? These people wanted blood and gore. This crap was the least I could offer.

When the war eventually ended, northern experiences began to emerge in torrents and folks from Kilinochchi, or Jaffna, or Paranthan would tell real hardship stories – of seeing friends gunned down in their sight, of spending countless nights in cramped bunkers, of mortars that came down around their ears like the monsoon. As so much of this was delivered in perfect deadpan, people like me would forever seem like monumental pansies. It was, I suppose, only fair.

Yet, although few could envy the circumstances which had shaped Elijah's youth, his neighbourhood had, as he suggested, escaped the very worst of war's ravages. Mannar lay on the fringes of the conflict; its lands had not been extensively mined, nor its buildings incessantly shelled. The war's most battered theatre lay east where I had just come from, past the newly repaired bridge, in the scrub and jungle of the Vanni.

At times, Mannar had even received refugees from these parts and, in this, there was a touch of historical irony.

Three-and-a-half centuries ago, it was a group from Mannar that had been besieged, and the Vanni that its residents had fled to. Finding solace in that wilderness, they founded Sri Lanka's most cherished Catholic church.

The first colonists who befell the island had, by most accounts, been the most vicious of the European invaders. In a particularly grim passage of his chronicle *Asia Portugeza*, Manuel de Faria e Sousa recounts the 'extraordinary cruelty' with which one Portuguese governor had sought to quell native defiance of their conquest.

> In the height of his success in Ceylon, [the governor] forced mothers to cast their children between millstones, and having seen them ground to mash, [the mothers] themselves were afterwards beheaded. He caused soldiers to take up children on the points of their pikes, and hearing them cry, bid them hark how those cocks crowed.... He caused many men to be cast off [a] bridge for the soldiers to see the crocodiles devour them. And those creatures were so used to this food that at a whistle they would lift their heads above water.

Nevertheless, though they terrorized Sri Lanka's traditional religions, took iron grip of the cinnamon trade, and wore trousers the size of hot-air balloons, the Portuguese did –

mostly inadvertently – enrich Sri Lankan life on a profound scale. It was them that, introduced the chilli to local kitchens, perhaps not anticipating that, in an ingenious reversal, the chilli would become Sri Lanka's most effective retaliatory weapon in the cutting down of Westerners. In the music of the Mozambican slaves they had shipped over were found the rhythms that birthed the beloved *baila*. And in turning swathes of the western coastal population to Catholicism, they added a fresh hue to Sri Lanka's religious palette. Even now, about nine per cent of the island remains faithful to their religion – my mother's extended family among them.

Eventually, however, the Dutch supplanted the Portuguese on the island's coasts and the new management was not enamoured of the religion their predecessors had left behind. Preferring their own particular brand of Christianity – Dutch Reformed – they made attempts to coerce the population into it, resorting often to violence and degradation of existing churches.

By 1670, the new colonists' intimidations had become unbearable to coastal Catholics and it is this persecution that our Mannar islanders had fled. About twenty families banded together, salvaged a prized statue of Mary from their church, and crossed the sea to the mainland. When they had left Dutch-controlled territory and passed into wilds within the bounds of the Kandyan Kingdom, they established a shrine at a crossroads called Madhu. Soon, 700 more Catholics fled south from Jaffna to join them. A critical mass of believers was reached. A tradition of Marian worship was set down. A community took root.

How exactly this far-flung forest outpost became one of Sri Lanka's most magnetic religious centres over the following centuries is not completely clear, but church's own oral history suggests it is because the shrine became reputed for supernatural healing.

What is beyond dispute, however, is that Madhu's appeal has transcended religious division for almost as long as the church has existed. Millions have visited the shrine; tens of thousands arriving annually. During the church's yearly feast in July, its fields overflow, not merely with Catholics from across the island, but with Hindus, Protestant Christians, and Buddhists. Some travel from as far as Matara and Hambantota, deep in the south.

For Elijah and me, the church had not taken much getting to. There was a forty-kilometre bus ride past Mannar's salt flats and on into the jungle on the same paved road I had come into town on, after which we disembarked at a three-way intersection, and looked for transportation that might ferry us a further ten kilometres north. Elijah did the haggling with the trishaw driver in Tamil and had us smoothly on our way. All that remained to me was to clamber in and watch the trees glide by.

The only unpleasantness, really, had been the ubiquity of military personnel. Even this long after war's end, the question of demilitarization remained a political hand grenade, and the government had balked at pulling the pin. We passed several bases: the 12th Gajaba Battallion, the 541st Infantry, the 54th Division, all with armed guards and solid steel gates flanked by hulking granite columns. The buildings belonging to residents – often one-room, NGO-funded shacks – cowered nearby.

Yet, when we arrived on the church premises, the politics melted into irrelevance. Somehow, Madhu did truly feel like a reprieve. On the sprawling grounds sat family groups in the shade of *veppei* and *alei* trees, sharing rice and curry that came out of stainless-steel tiffin sets. Old men ambled around on the lawn, inspecting a series of statues that depicted Christ's crucifixion; little girls in long dresses chased each other around the plinths nearby. From the canopies surrounding the clearing, a host of chirps abounded.

The church itself rose in cream and light blue – no high-flying cathedral to be sure but imposing enough for a building so remote. Inside, two burnished colonnades ran on either side of a nave enclosed by dark banisters and hymnal-turning gusts swept through wide-open rows of wooden doors. Gazing maternally over the pilgrims from a glass case above the altar was Our Lady of Madhu – Mary, in a dazzling turquoise gown, clutching the Christ child tight to her breast. She looked well for her age, three-and-a-half centuries since her rescue from the Dutch. Writ upon the wood panel below her, a prayer: 'Grant our country permanent peace.'

She had been among those spared when the church was attacked in November of 1999. Forty Vanni residents who had come to seek her refuge had not been so lucky. The full truth of that evening's tragedy has, as ever, been obscured by the whirl of tit-for-tat propaganda that characterized the conflict:

the government announcing LTTE had launched their mortars, the LTTE claiming army tanks had laid the siege, no conclusive evidence having emerged either way.

And still, it was congruence – not conflict – that struck me, as I sat in the back pews with Elijah. Before us, on the floor, were gathered devotees in little clumps, reading prayers from weathered missals. In their pious, unified murmur I heard strains of the Hindu mantras that had spilled out of hill country kovils. The groups of women dressed in white, legs folded beside them, may as well have been at the tooth relic in Kandy, or beneath the Jaya Sri Maha Bodhi. Their prayers for the safety of their husbands, for the healing of the sick, for favourable exam results, and for the fertility of their children were all familiar refrains now.

Even Muslims – historically the most isolated of Sri Lanka's religious communities – have been longtime pilgrims here. British adventurer John Still had chronicled a little of Madhu's ecumenical appeal in 1930:

> In the very middle of the forest, hidden farther from cities than any other church in Ceylon, there is an old Roman Catholic mission, so catholic indeed that men and women of all creeds flock there on pilgrimage, and I have even known a strict Mahomedan to go there from Anuradhapura, carrying with him his sick baby son in full faith that he would be healed there.

While we sat, Elijah told me of the reverence with which some local Catholics held the church, and here, there was more resonance. When news broke that Madhu had fallen into the army's hands in 2008, Catholic LTTE supporters had become demoralized, believing the losing of the war to have become almost inevitable. Almost two centuries ago, the British capture of the Buddha's tooth had had a near identical effect on Keppetipola's hill country rebellion – the loss of the relic described by one Kandyan aristocrat as 'infinitely more important' to the failure of that struggle than even the eventual arrest and deaths of its leaders. A sense of haunting destiny pervaded each event: if the relic is gone, or the church has been taken, perhaps it is meant to be this way.

Of all the things I had expected from the Vanni, frankly, concord had not been one. How could it have been? This was the most warred-over strap of the country, forming the age-old borderland between Sinhala and Tamil strongholds. Thousands of years before gunfire and claymores consumed the last generation, royals had pitched savage battles here upon elephant back. Surrendered, retaken, and lost again, have been these forests. Endlessly displaced have been its people, shaped profoundly by violence their lives.

And yet how this sanctuary has thrived. When Sri Lankans converge on Madhu, they find their differences stripped away. All that remains is elemental: aspirations shared by every race, hopes that are common to all. Deep in the jungle, amid battlefields ancient and modern, here is another of Sri Lanka's mystifying delights: the most unlikely outpost of common ground.

NINE

Shoots of Peace

Nowhere on the island can you get where you are going quite as smoothly as you can in the Vanni. Two reasons, one of them unhappy. This being the poorest belt of the country, there are few cars, vans, lorries, or trishaws with which the roads might be crammed. Then there is the state of the tarmac itself: wide, charcoal grey, and pothole free – much of it having been rebuilt since the war's end.

There is also the illusion of rapid movement. Where in hulking landmasses such as India, or the United States, you might travel for hours and barely have budged on the map, in Sri Lanka you need only skim along for half an hour before a fresh locale bounds up to greet you. Nowhere is this truer than in the Vanni, where the island tapers to its skinny neck. Whenever I checked the map on my northern travels, the blue dot that represented my location was flinging itself purposefully across the phone screen.

I was now on the coastal road heading north. Following the visit to Madhu, I had returned to Mannar to pick up my things, then immediately boarded this bus, which hurtled back over the bridge and swung left past some salt flats. Forty minutes into the journey, Mannar town already seemed a distant memory, new, unfamiliar scenes having materialized outside the bus window. Early on, the most prominent building in a passing village had been the Catholic church (usually painted blue, as Madhu had been). Further north, the red-and-white pinstripe wall of the kovil began to impose itself. The earth was also red: stereotypically east African, perhaps because this strip of the island had once rubbed up against Madagascar, all those millions of years ago. In between long stretches of scrub, broad acacia canopies brooded over tall, dry grass, and plots of farmland lay dormant, awaiting the monsoon rains that might defibrillate them back into life. In the hamlets, dark, slim women in colourful saris shuffled on the roadsides, and spindly men stood idle in the storefronts.

But such is the Vanni's inclination, that before I became familiar with one set of sights, the scenery transformed again. A mangrove forest appeared, then another – evening rays glinting off the brackish water. Soon, a long bridge transported us over ocean, and we passed into land hemmed in on one side by saltwater inlets.

When in the dusk, I saw the outlines of a multitude of palmyrah – their long thin trunks rising straight, then bursting into a distinctive sphere of palm branches – I knew I had arrived in the northern peninsula. Within an hour, I had dragged my now-filthy bags into a guesthouse and fallen into bed.

Growing up, it seemed like every adult in the Kochchikade neighbourhood of Negombo, had at some point in their youth, received a beating from my grandmother.

These had been delivered at her after-school tuition classes that students from miles around had flocked to. Though my grandmother had retired before I was born, her old students would often drop by for a cup of tea. Having made the normal inquiries about her health, they would soon take a moment to recall her acts of violence.

'Foo! Fransisca miss, I still remember that blistering whack you gave me one day while I was sitting at that table,' the student would say, grinning and gesturing towards the furniture. 'The moment you saw me copying spelling words from my sister, *pataas*! – the shot came here, straight to my ear. I still get scared thinking about it. I think the ear is still ringing also.'

The purpose here was to raise a nostalgic chuckle from my grandmother. But although among family she could be jovial, she never dropped the headmistress act with her former students.

'And how many marks did you get in your next test? I remember clearly that you came first in your class.' (No student of hers, she insisted, had ever failed to come first.) At this point, she would set off on a long, regretful monologue about not having been stern enough with her pupils. The implication was that Kochchikade would now be swimming with astronauts and famous inventors if only her beatings had been greater in volume and brutality.

She never could bring herself to hit her own grandchildren, though in my case she should probably have considered it. Once, when I had brought home a report that placed me seventh in the class, she remarked there was no point in parents sending children to school if they could not at least come in the top three. Insolent little prick that I was, I had told her to feel free to unenrol me.

Another time, I had insisted through the holidays that I had not been assigned homework, but on the last night of the break, sprung on her that I had ten workbook pages to complete. If I think on that evening, I can still hear her scolding. But, irate as she seemed at the time, she stayed up and helped me through every last exercise. Is it not wonderful that no matter how prickly or hard-nosed somebody is, they will always save the softest parts of themselves for their grandchildren?

One of my grandmother's favourite complaints to us kids in those days was that we never took our education seriously enough and it was at these times that the north's largest town was invoked. 'You children, playing all day and wasting all your talents away, you should see how the children in Jaffna study,' she'd cluck. She had attended training college in Jaffna in the 1940s. 'Jaffna is a place where they know the value of hard work, ah. Every night the children are at their desks with their schoolbooks. And unlike you spoiled ones, they probably have to study by lamp light. See how clever they are – how well Jaffna Tamils are doing abroad.'

Growing up in the southern two thirds of the country in the 1990s, a lot of what you heard about Jaffna was that there were folks up there who ran around with bombs strapped to their chests, looking for busloads of innocent people to blow up. But even at the height of fighting, the one concession southern folk would make was that northerners were, in general, an industrious and cerebral people. How could they not be? The most famous edifice in Jaffna – and once the pride of the town – was their library. In fact, in gutting that building with fire in 1981, the government-sponsored mob had intentionally struck Jaffna where it would leave the angriest welt. The library has since been resurrected, glorious Indo-Saracenic dome and all, though without the priceless trove of palm-leaf manuscripts that had been sent up in flames that night. Even in this depleted second life, it is perhaps the only library in the country where you are asked to remove footwear before entering – a requirement otherwise reserved for places of worship.

There is also thought to be a pace and an ambition about Jaffna that is uncommon elsewhere on the island. I guess you would have to spend a few months in the city to really work out whether that was true. What I did happily notice the next morning, was how well the town centre seemed to have sprung back from war. In my one previous trip to the city in 2013, the place had been scattered with derelict houses – roofless, overgrown, and with bullet wounds dressing the surviving walls. Now, old lots had been spruced up, licks of fresh paint had been applied, the last of the wartime kerosene-fuelled cars had vanished, and shiny Japanese and

Indian automobiles had taken their place on the streets. In evidence, also, was a spanking new four-star hotel (now the tallest building in town), brightly-tiled supermarkets, a swish new cineplex, and well-tended public parks.

But if the roaring Jaffna ambition of stereotype was driving this growth, that is not to say the city lacked a sense of humour, particularly about itself. During my stay, I came by a charming homegrown story about the Jaffna state of mind. It went like this:

A wealthy Sheikh was visiting Jaffna when, one day, he gets into a major accident and needs a very rare type of blood for an operation. The hospital scours the region and after some delay finds a Jaffna man with a matching blood type. The local takes a little convincing, but as the Sheikh's life is on the line, agrees to make a donation.

When the man returns home from the hospital, he finds, to his great delight, a host of gifts from the Sheikh. There is a gold watch, jewellery for his wife, toys for his children, and even a luxury car for the family. Overjoyed, he begins to flaunt his new wealth around the neighbourhood.

A few days later, he gets a message that while the Sheikh's surgery had been successful, the doctors require just a little more of his blood for a small, but important secondary procedure. This time, the man volunteers immediately, expecting another round of gifts.

But a week after this second donation, the man has not received so much as a thank you note. He is crestfallen. He begins to complain to friends and neighbours about the Sheikh's ingratitude and is eventually convinced to confront the Sheikh directly.

'What is the meaning of this?' he asks, having tracked down the Sheikh's number. 'First time you shower me with presents, and this time you can't even thank me?'

'Yes, but you must understand,' the Sheikh replies, 'now I have Jaffna blood in my veins.'

Isn't that terrific? Although, I could not help but feel the story was unkind to Jaffna's residents. Folks up here were not quite as laidback as residents of the south perhaps, and certainly not like they had been in Mannar. But right through my stay I would encounter the same generosity of spirit that had made the remainder of Sri Lanka such a joy. Homes would be opened to me and help made bountifully available. On the occasions I revealed I was working on a book, I was even made to feel quite important – much more than I deserved. 'Ah, you are wanting to write about Jaffna,' would come the exclamation. 'I know this old sir who has lived here all his life. Knows everything there is to know about the area and speaks perfect English also. Here, come, I'll give you his number. In fact, you know what, come to my place and have something to eat. Afterwards I will take you. How do you like prawn curry?'

And so, the first scorching day in Jaffna became filled with fascinating conversation and harrowing wartime stories, both of which the town has an inexhaustible seam. One old gentleman told me of the daily humiliations of military occupation: 'These young fellows in their combat uniforms – Tigers or army they were all the same – got such a big, bloody head when they got a gun in their hand. They would have been in their nappies when I was working my first job, but you should have seen the way the buggers would treat me.

Shouting and shouting about freedom, but no one had taught them one ounce of humanity. Once, I remember handing over some documents because I needed to travel out to get some medicine. If you believe it, they threw the file across the floor and laughed while I picked up the papers.'

My guesthouse owner Dinesh, whose family had lived just southeast of Jaffna through much of the fighting, recalled some of the LTTE's recruitment drives: 'My friends and I used to play football in one of the fields near home. Probably every few months, an LTTE cadre would turn up and ask us to come to their brainwashing seminars. They showed us planes they had shot down and said we could also be heroes. One of my good friends, Ruban, joined. I never heard from him again.'

Virtually everyone I met, too, had been displaced by the fighting at some point. Those fortunate enough to return to their properties – often months later – would find their houses either destroyed, or at the very least, shot up and ransacked, landmines planted where the flowerpots had been. When, during wartime, even the most basic goods – books, medicines, building materials – had to be shipped in at vastly inflated costs, people came to understand that their own lives were dirt. One wrong move – a careless word to a vengeful military man, or an errant artillery shell – could end lives and leave families destitute.

Yet, it was with a bracing freedom that Jaffna locals retold their difficult stories. Generally, no questions were left unanswered. My monumental ignorance about the northern wartime plight was graciously tolerated. Before long, it began to dawn on me that the economic boom was something of a mirage – indebtedness, unemployment, and poverty still rife on the outskirts of town and beyond it. Yet, even those with little to give remained unfailingly generous with their time and their belongings. One family insisted on lending me a bicycle, though they could barely spare it. When I offered to leave money as a guarantee for its return, they refused.

I suppose, just like with any city, not all its residents could be completely above board. Yet, even the trishaw drivers who quoted exorbitant prices upon realizing I was an outsider, did so with a dazzling smile and a winning wink, and I have always found those such endearing traits in people who are trying to fleece me.

As dusk fell on my first full day in Jaffna, I was paid a visit by G. Gopikrishna, whom I had befriended on that previous visit. A tall man, with a builder's shoulders and an action-hero moustache, Gopi was a longtime English teacher and a lifelong sports nut. As such, he had a habit of speaking liberally in cricket parlance. He had not merely had a birthday in the last few months, he was '40 not out'. He was not only content with his longtime job at Jaffna's St John's College, he was 'batting on a good pitch' there.

'You must be finding Jaffna very much changed,' he said, leaning back on the rattan-weave chair in the verandah of my guesthouse.

'I am. It's incredible.' I myself had often told visitors to Colombo of my city's rapid transformation, so recognized a little of the pride in Gopi's words.

'Next time you return, it will be even more different,' he said. 'I have lived here all my life, but I can definitely say now that things are moving forwards. Development has come to Jaffna.'

Gopi was something of an optimist – maybe even unreasonably so. Not for him were grouses about past injustices committed by Sinhalese or complaints about ongoing discrimination. His Jaffna, which for so much of his life had been strung up by the violence, had finally gained its freedom and lay bristling with promise and opportunity. The Nallur kovil, where he has long worshipped, could at last set about beautifying its spectacular burnt-orange *gopuram* and touching up its interior artwork. His beloved St John's College was now in a position to build a swimming pool, even if the building committee, of which he was a member, had 'too many captains', which was slowing the project down.

'You see, people must understand the government situation,' he said when talk had turned to politics, and I'd asked him if enough was being done to rebuild the north. 'It is not like a Twenty20. It is a Test match. We have to keep batting and play a long innings.'

This was a little cryptic even for me, so I asked him to explain.

'We can't expect solutions to all the problems at one time, no? Ok, I will give you an example. There are very many people who are upset that the army is still holding the lands they took over during the war – that they are not releasing it to the people. But we should realize slowly, slowly that is also happening. Two months back, the army gave back hundred acres near Palaly area. I have friends who will make a big fuss and say the government is not doing this, and not doing that, but I told them: "Wait. Have some patience. Good things will come."'

Such arguments with friends he seemed to have had plenty of in recent weeks. Jaffna has never quite been the political monolith many southerners believed it to be but this week I had caught the town in a particularly divided frame of mind. This was because, just the previous month, Jaffna had hosted an 8,000-strong political rally named Eluga Tamil – Eluga meaning 'rise up'. Of the demonstrators' demands, some – such as the insistence on demilitarization of their lands – were reasonable. Others, like the call for the prevention of Sinhalese settlement in the north, were controversial, bordering on racist. The political waves the hardline rally had generated were a source of frustration for northern moderates.

'I mean, you only have to look at who had organized this rally,' Gopi said, sitting forward in his chair now. 'People want to move on, but certain disaffected politicians are trying to stir trouble.'

'Disaffected how?' I asked.

'See, some of those organizers didn't win a seat in the last election. They don't care whether Jaffna develops or not. They only want to be in power.'

'But they still managed to get a lot of attention, didn't they?'

'You know, it's always the radicalists that shout the loudest.'

I suppose this is true of the politics everywhere but is particularly the case in Sri Lanka, where moderatism has had a history of under-representation in the national dialogue. Social anthropologist Jonathan Spencer has referred to nationalism in Sri Lanka as an 'over-production' – ideas pitched at a volume outsize to their actual influence over the population. The north has at times dealt with its moderates in especially chilling fashion. In the LTTE's early years, it had first silenced Tamil voices that sought peaceful resolutions to grievances, before it properly set its sights on the government. Sometimes threats and intimidation had been enough. Often, if they persisted, dissenting men and women were killed off.

The moderates' plight has not been helped, either, by the smug hordes of Western journalists who have descended on the island for their two-week assignments, got scene-setting shots of war-torn places, interviewed the crazies on either side, painted those men (they are often men) as leading representatives of their communities, then delivered anguished verdicts about the hopelessness of it all – much of it with the kind of moral certitude that has eluded Sri Lankans who have wrestled with these problems for decades. It seems inconceivable that when these people went to return home they were able to fit themselves and their belongings on the same aeroplanes, so vast was the profusion of self-righteousness they had acquired during the exercise.

Perhaps you are a Western journalist and, reading this, feel I am over-generalizing or being glib. Good. Now you know what that feels like.

At any rate, I could sympathize with Gopi, who wanted to believe that Jaffna was not on a return route to violence. He was doing what he could to protect his city's fragile calm.

'Some of my friends actually wanted to go to the rally,' he lamented. 'I was asking them: "What will you achieve by going there? What do you want to do? You want to start the war again? You will start the match and run away abroad. Other people who are stuck here only will have to play the match."'

And with that, he had touched on yet another truth about Sri Lankan war-making that resonates through the ages. Elites conceive and control the direction of the conflict. The poorest almost always find themselves at the nasty end of the gun or the spear. Jaffna, being the Tamil intellectual hub, and the most prosperous pocket of the region, was in a sense the northern Colombo, but with that came a casual disdain for the less privileged – the caste system uniquely persisting here to such an extent that, in some places, tar seal gave out to potholes or gravel the moment the road entered a low-caste neighbourhood. Indifferently treated, too, were Jaffna's minorities. Moor Street, where many Muslims lived, languished still in a state of relative disrepair while the remainder of the city picked itself up around the enclave.

Eventually, Gopi and I had had enough of the political chatter. It had sapped the joy out of our meeting. It had turned each of us morose. But when we decided to change the subject, talk only turned to the prospects of the Sri Lankan cricket team, which was no less depressing a topic. Ours had been a doomed conversation, really.

A little later, he mounted his motorbike and set off for a meeting about the school pool, hollering: 'What to do but keep the faith?'

The next day I would encounter more of the sort of

nationalism Gopi had lamented. I'd be reminded that for all the war-fatigued folk tending the shoots of Sri Lanka's young peace, destructive enmities persisted.

If there is one thing Jaffna locals cherish more than their library, more than their traditions, more even than religion, it is their tongue.

And why not? It is a marvel.

With a written history stretching 2,500 years, Tamil is one of the planet's longest-surviving languages and almost nowhere else has a more classical form of it been preserved than on the peninsula. This is largely why Sri Lanka's post-independence assaults on their language had been so repugnant to the north, plunging the nation, in fits, towards war. Fair to say, no more calamitous legislation has ever been passed on the island than the Sinhala Only Act of 1956.

Sadly, this was of little help to me because I have the Tamil competence of a cowbell. Growing up, my mother had never really spoken it at home and I had never made the effort to pick up more than the most basic words and phrases from her relatives, who anyway spoke Sinhala and English with ease. Before my visit I had wondered if this ignorance of the northern language would inhibit me here; I worried I would struggle to make myself understood.

On this score I found myself surprised because an ironic consequence of the conflict had been that more Jaffna residents spoke Sinhala now than ever. Hordes of northerners had sought refuge from the fighting in India and the global West, of course, but a large proportion had also fled south, to Colombo, or Kandy, or Nuwara Eliya. Many of those that remained on the island had since returned to a peaceful Jaffna, ferrying back functional iterations of the southern tongue. Sometimes, the Sinhala came from further afield: I met a trishaw driver who had learned it in Qatar, where his colleagues at a diesel garage had been southerners. In being pieced back together, Jaffna was finding itself mottled in all sorts of unexpected shades.

I, meanwhile, discovered novel failures in my own ability to communicate, even in the languages that I did possess. Despite its recent proliferation, Sinhala was still far from ubiquitous in the city, so when I needed to ask a question, I would generally venture it in English first, in order to avoid coming off as a southern prat who demanded northerners converse in the majority tongue (English, being of foreign origin, was neutral territory). On the many occasions my English was not understood, I would attempt to change to Sinhala and it was at this point that my circuits would malfunction. I realized in Jaffna that I do not switch smoothly. Generally, there would be several empty seconds while my system rebooted in a new language – the waiter or bystander I was addressing made to stand awkwardly before me. The first burst of Sinhala would always come out garbled and spliced with accidental English words. When this mish-mash splutter persisted – smoke now billowing out of my ears – the other person would become convinced I was having a stroke. Only when the ambulance arrived did I usually regain some semblance of intelligibility.

Thankfully, Jaffna residents were bright enough to offset my shortcomings and, the next morning, an older trishaw driver caught the Tamil place name in Sinhala–English jumble I had spewed at him and soon had us skimming north on another of the peninsula's bright new roads. As I sat back, a warm wind began to buffet me. The paddies that materialized outside were white and dusty, more desiccated here than elsewhere. Even the ever-defiant stubble of grass and weeds seemed to have been pulverized by the Jaffna sun. Tips of the palmyrah fronds had yellowed. The entire landscape begged for relief.

When we turned westwards at the village of Chunnakam, the road itself seemed to become sapped of energy, narrowing suddenly just before it delivered us to our destination. Bordered on all sides by a fence and overlooked by copses of palmyrah, one of Sri Lanka's most-ancient religious sites was guarded by a machine-gun wielding army man. It was no surprise the place had been co-opted in the churning madness that was Sri Lanka's racial politics.

I didn't even know how to refer to the place, really. Was it Kandarodai, which was the Tamil name of the hamlet that enclosed it? Or Kadurugoda, as a Sinhala chronicle from the middle ages had it? Whatever the case, it was an ancient Buddhist *viharaya* (temple), about two dozen brickwork bases of 2,300-year old dagoba having been found here when it was originally re-discovered in 1917. On some bases, stupas had since been rebuilt with matte grey coral stone – none to stand taller than a standard doorway. On the ground, aluminum signs – white lettering on black paint – numbered off each structure.

Fascinatingly, though the ruins are Buddhist, archaeologists have suggested that the settlement at Kandarodai had been Tamil – the second and third century BC potsherds discovered there having borne Tamil-Brahmi scripts. Adding further weight to this theory, a coin unearthed from one of the lower layers had also borne the image of the Hindu goddess Lakshmi, suggesting an easy commerce with South India.

Now here is where the politics intrudes. While for any sane person it is a thing of small wonder that some early Buddhists could have been Tamil, that thought is completely unpalatable to the chauvinist from the south. For him Sri Lankan Buddhists are now, and have always been, Sinhalese and Sinhalese alone. Moreover, no Dravidians could possibly have been on the island roughly 2,300 years ago, when the first Sinhalese kingdoms were establishing themselves. Sri Lanka was not so much a country in their minds but an ice cream cone first licked by the Sinhalese; anyone else seeking to enjoy it needed to conform to their terms. So instead of any honest, scholarly appraisal of the site's possible past, what I found at Kandarodai was a Sinhala banner that referred to the place only by its Sinhala name. It proclaimed the ruins a 'witness to the glorious history of Sinhalese-Buddhism'.

My mind returned to the torture tree at Paranagama, where Sinhalese villagers had died in a clear-cut atrocity committed by a foe who thought himself racially superior but where no memorial of any kind stood. At Kandarodai instead was the kind of pseudo-history Sri Lanka believed in – the kind that put the nation constantly at odds with itself and pit local races against one another.

But although it was this southern strain of nationalism that posed the greatest threat to national unity, tacitly approved as it was by the state, this is not to say Tamil nationalists did not themselves possess an equally perverted version of history to justify their own supposed primacy. At the library that afternoon, I came upon a 2006 book published by Jaffna University entitled *Tamil Civilization: The Untold History*, written by a V. Navaratnam. The author, it turned out, had once been a member of the nation's parliament between 1963 and 1970. A fairly influential lawyer and Jaffna intellectual he had been as well.

For him, the Sinhalese were not a distinct people but had once been Tamils, until they 'fell victim' to Buddhist missionaries and split off from the parent race. Their language, also, was not descended from the North Indian Sanskrit, but was itself a daughter tongue of Tamil. Where both claims aim to present the Sinhalese as subordinate, neither, of course, stands up to even the most cursory academic scrutiny.

On display here was a Tamil counterweight to the resounding stupidity encountered at Kandarodai. Just as with the Sinhala equivalent, a magnificent past was called up, a proud religion was invoked, and two-and-a-half-thousand years of history, culture, and tradition, warped just so, was harnessed for the benefit of the pettiest of arguments – the most small-minded claims of supremacy.

I had come to realisze that without one, perhaps the other would not exist. The nationalists of one side needed the opposite set of racists to be hale and rowdy, else there would be little reason to rouse the public up. On the surface, Sinhala and Tamil nationalists stood at disparate ends of the spectrum. At their core, they were one another's great allies.

I chose to forget the politics during my last thirty-six hours in Jaffna. I fulfilled a childhood ambition instead. Taking a bus west, over water, I travelled to the northern archipelago that had intrigued me since I had first spotted it on the map and found it as fascinating as I'd imagined: each island so flat and low-lying – so much like paper dosa on a griddle – I almost expected to be able to reach down to the beaches and peel each landmass up off the sea.

The road there, too, was unlike any other I had seen. It went from island to island to island on increasingly slim causeways, until the final stretch over water was on such a thin strand of concrete, the bus practically tiptoed along it, turquoise waves sploshing about on either side. Along the way were lands so ocean-bleached that even the air tasted of salt; matchbox kovils with multicolour gopuram no taller than a cabinet; outcrops of palmyrah, which grew thinner and shorter here than on the mainland; and dozens of dark men fishing open-shirted, with beat-up nets, egrets flitting about the shallows around them.

On the sixth island I had been on that day, called Kurikadduwan, the road ended, and from there, I hopped aboard a diesel-powered barge that would ferry me a few hundred metres to a seventh: Nainatheevu. There postured a Buddhist viharaya and a tall Hindu kovil. On this day it was the viharaya that was better attended – a busload of pilgrims chanting beneath a seaside bodhi – but both places of worship drew adherents from far and wide. The viharaya because this island is said to have been visited by the Buddha; the kovil because it featured in the Mahabharata.

My final morning in the city I decided to spend eating. Jaffna, I had found, was a culinary fantasyland. Where the southern curries I had been weaned on were intricately spiced – flavours coming through one by one, like a series of visitors on a cool afternoon – northern cuisine scoffed at the whole idea of subtlety, practically tearing down the front door to take tastebuds hostage. Wholeheartedly did mine surrender. I gorged on Jaffna's blazing crab curries, feasted on rich mutton dishes, and slurped down hearty bowls of *odiyal kool* soup.

And here's something I had known even before this visit, but bears a little shouting about: there is no tastier fruit in existence than the Jaffna *karuthacolomban* mango, and I will argue that to all comers. Now, there are some folks – call them fruit hipsters – who contend that karuthacolomban is overrated and will instead suggest that *vilad* or *gira* varieties are superior. These people are idiots. There is a reason why the karuthacolomban is the most famous varietal. Subscribing to a contrary opinion does not automatically put a person on a higher intellectual plane.

As a child, I learned northern geography from the evening news. 'Seventeen Tigers and nine army personnel were killed when fighting erupted overnight near Vavuniya.' Helpfully, a map of Sri Lanka would pop up, and a blinking red bauble would indicate the location of the battleground.

My Sinhalese grandfather was a religious viewer of the 7 pm news and it was to the war reports he paid the most attention. He would always sit in the same rattan-weave armchair, hushing us kids when the opening graphics came on, leaning forward, limbs tense, as the day's body count was read out. Almost never were government casualties reported to be higher than the Tigers' and I sensed in him a satisfaction that that was the case. But then the war segment would end and a forlorn look would descend. Settling back into his chair, he would let out a great sigh. Every day he would mumble some variation of the same thing: 'Terrible thing, no, this war? Whoever they are fighting for, they are all somebody's son or daughter, isn't it? Just imagine. All human lives. Our very own people.'

Thanks to the daily reports, northern place names were more familiar to me in those days than those of some Colombo suburbs. I had heard more about Kilinochchi than Kotte; I could point out Point Pedro but was less sure where Pelawatte might be found. Of the northern locations, however, none commanded the airwaves like Elephant Pass. This is the central isthmus that controls access to Jaffna's peninsula, and as such, had been a particularly vaunted prize of the conflict. Thousands had died in the constant fighting in its vicinity. Boats had been sunk in the water, mortars had been launched across the expanse, grenades had been lobbed, and millions of rounds liberally fired.

That evening, as the bus rode south on the one-kilometre causeway over Elephant Pass, I was astonished to find the place overrun with serenity. Fishing canoes bobbed in hesitant waves. Painted storks waded in pink-and-amber shallows – the water reflecting a bewitching sunset. Could this really be Elephant Pass? I found the place impossible to reconcile with its history.

Kilinochchi, however, posed no such challenge. The bus had got in after nightfall but when I saw the town properly next morning, it was obvious this had been a war-devastated place. Where Sri Lankan towns left to their own devices tend to develop winding dead-end lanes, curious horseshoe corners, and endlessly complex subdivisions, so much of Kilinochchi's roads and buildings served a clear-cut purpose. Here was the bank, next door was the hardware store, and there was the barber just beyond it. All sat on their own clearly-marked plots of land, each building so new; no eatery had sprouted in the basement, nor a bicycle shop from a side annexe. Instead of being clustered around a central roundabout or intersection, Kilinochchi was oriented lengthways as if a normal town had been scooped up then scraped off along the sides of the vast Jaffna–Kandy highway. Decades may pass before the town musters up the population and economy to match the heft of its central road.

Nevertheless, the place thrummed with a restless energy, even on this Sunday morning. Tamil pop songs tumbled out of the speakers outside a little communication shop, a slender fellow hawked lotto tickets under an awning, and a soldier paced the pavements with a Kalashnikov slung under his arm.

No one paid him the slightest attention and I suppose this was unsurprising. As the LTTE's old administrative capital, the town had seen some of the most ferocious battles of the war, not least in the months preceding government capture in January 2009. On a global list of places unfazed by men wielding automatic weapons, Kilinochchi would have to be top ten.

By the time I made my way outdoors, the stupendous heat of the Vanni had gripped the town and, soon, every movement was an effort. It was the most oppressive day of the trip yet – the kind of weather to which the only appropriate response might be to lay immobile under a million fans. But as I intended to spend no more than a few hours here, I forced myself to get out and explore. I wanted to find a war monument I had seen the previous evening. Though my flip flops were slippery with perspiration and I was more or less a human sprinkler, I began to trudge through town at about 10 am.

Eventually, sodden-shirted, I arrived at the monument: a toppled water tower, which even in the darkness of the night before had seemed imposing from my bus window. Close up and in broad daylight, it was downright gigantic. A lorry could have driven through the tower's hollowed-out body, which lay mostly intact. It spanned about two bus lengths end-to-end – effectively a tunnel, in this horizontal orientation. At the end that faced away from the road, the hulking concrete cylinder mushroomed out into a vast reservoir. This is where the majority of the tower's 1.5 million litres of water would have been stored before the explosives were strapped to the tower's base and it was made to keel over. The LTTE had wrought this devastation, the government said. A marble plaque stood nearby, reading:

'This fallen tower … the source of water for the people … destroyed by LTTE terrorists in the face of valiant troops converging on Kilinochchi in January 2009 … is a silent witness to the brutality of terrorism … a monument to the futility of terror …' and on in such fashion.

Around the plaque stood a family: southerners, who were part of a tour group that had alighted their charter bus just as I had arrived. Perhaps because I had barely spoken in over a day, I struck up a conversation.

'Where are you folks coming from?' I asked in Sinhala.

'We're on our way back home to Ampara, actually,' a man of middle years replied. 'We were in the peninsula yesterday.'

'What did you think of Jaffna town?' I ventured. 'Coming up nicely, isn't it?'

'Really? See, well, we actually didn't get to look at much of the town.'

'How come?'

'We came for the pilgrimage, no? All of yesterday we were in Nagadeepa viharaya, and then we went to Dambakola Patuna temple. No time, with all of that.'

I should have guessed, really. This was the shape southern tourism to the north had taken in the post-war years. There were, of course, many small groups who had arrived on the train or a public bus and taken in the region's many treasures as normal tourists might. But the leading convention by far was to band together in a crowd of thirty or more and shuttle up the A9 to visit only the sites that resonated with southerners

– mainly historic Buddhist temples, but also war monuments such as this.

And where, by rights, southern tourism should at the very least prove an economic boon to locals, it had become apparent that this was rarely the case. It was not local-owned joints the buses usually stopped at but military-run restaurants where waiters spoke the southern tongue and served southern fare. When the tourists needed to bunk down for a night, military-operated rest camps were again preferred – this particular group having stayed at a Navy-run place on the northern edge of the peninsula. In coming to the north, it had become common, for reasons of convenience and affordability, to visit only the Sinhalese enclaves within it.

Soon, an Army man in combat fatigues trotted around the site to summon the crowd to the souvenir shop. Addressing the gathering, he told us about the final Battle of Kilinochchi – how the forces had pressed the town from three directions, how they had been rebuffed three times in the last months of 2008 while monsoon floods stymied their advance, and how, with time, the LTTE had been worn down and overcome. The terrible price men and women of the military paid for peace was repeatedly stressed.

Unmentioned was the cataclysm the conflict had wreaked upon the northern populace. On whether local civilians in the poorest belt of the island were recovering, there was not a word.

I caught a bus headed south out of Kilinochchi that afternoon and, a few hours after that, had stopped off at Vavuniya and boarded another due to leave for the northeast coast. As I exited the north, the war felt like something Sri Lankans still saw as having waged on each other. One day, perhaps, they will not so casually spurn the chance to understand the humans who had been on the other side. Maybe eventually, Sri Lankans will learn to see the war like my grandfather had: as a horror that they, together, endured.

TEN

The Dolki Drum People

I first saw Trincomalee from a boat. The town shimmered in the early sun; the dainty pastel shades of its low-slung buildings separated from the ocean's cobalt by an ivory beach.

I had not had a good look at the place when I had arrived the previous day because by then it was already dark. Not only had the bus taken much longer to depart Vavuniya than advertised, the driver and conductor had then also decided to disappear into a roadside rice-and-curry joint halfway through our journey, leaving paying customers to brine in sweat and discontent for a further thirty minutes. I sensed a growing restlessness in my fellow passengers, but no one dared confront the bus operators. Of Sri Lanka's great propensity to quietly tolerate inconvenience, I have written a haiku:

Yes, I'm unhappy,
But I'm too scared to complain,
Can't somebody else?

At any rate, the bus did deliver us without further incident to Trinco, and for that I should be grateful. The place was an out-and-out paradise.

The town itself was one of the more interesting of its size in the island, lively little hodgepodge store fronts crowding characterful lanes, as Tamil pop tunes pulsed through the alleyways. Across from the main bus station, Arafa Hotel served up tasty northeastern curries atop mountains of rice, while street vendors hawked Muslim sweets, and *kadalai*.

There was even – and I am not kidding here – a resident population of spotted deer traipsing around the streets, descendants, supposedly, of a breeding pair that had been brought to the nearby Fort Frederick during the last decades of British rule. When, later on that first day, I came into town, I spotted signs urging folks to 'refrain from littering with polythene in order to conserve the deer population', and then saw a stag, velvet antlers and all, begging for food and water in the doorway of a sari shop. Even for a country in which monkeys, dogs, five-foot monitor lizards, cows, snakes, donkeys, and occasionally elephants, patrol urban spaces, this was pure nonsense. Was there any species that would fail to proliferate in Sri Lanka? Get those skinny polar bears off their disappearing ice floes and ship them to the island, I say. Within months they would be pestering passersby for food, darting out in front of enraged trishaw drivers, and crapping lavishly all over the pavements.

But for all the town's low-key appeal, it was the beaches and the ocean that were Trinco's greater enchantments. That first morning, after passing the town by sea, our boat found two pods of spinner dolphins. Despite the din from our outboard motor, they performed for us their acrobatics, leaping two metres into the air to whirl like dervishes. Soon, a juvenile blue whale joined the show. It sent up a spout fifty metres away to spark mass excitement among the flotilla of tourists that had now gathered. Diving with a flick of its tail whenever a boat drew close, it announced its return to the surface with another spout, minutes later, fifty metres in a different direction.

Later in the day, Erena arrived following a long bus ride from Colombo, and we checked into a fancy hotel for another forty-eight hours of opulence. It was glorious. We ate our body weight in *kiri bath* (coconut milk rice-cake), aappa, and pancakes at the breakfast buffet, then lay around in hammocks slung between seaside coconut trees, heading every now and then into the ocean for a dip. On the beach, a gang of weather-beaten local fishermen hauled their *maadala* (great net) in from the shallows, legs, hips, and arms all working in well-rehearsed unison. Out in deeper water, several white boats belonging to a Colombo-based sailing club tacked and tilted across the waves.

On the second day, we rode a boat to Pigeon Island, which lies a few hundred metres from the coast, and snorkeled among a multitude of unremittingly dazzling tropical fish: oriental sweetlips with their racing stripes, schools of bannerfish with their filament fins, boxfish with polka-dot bonnets, and the especially memorable picasso triggerfish – their rear halves clubbed with colour, their front ends tapering to a sombre, surrealist snout. And that was only the northern side. Off the island's southern beach grew a ravishing field of green-and-blue table coral, in which prowled, near the ocean floor, three-metre long white-tipped reef sharks – dangerous only to marine life, supposedly, but still so sleek, still so menacing, human hearts could not help but thud in quivering ears.

Then, in the blink of an eye, it ended. Erena boarded a train back to Colombo, and our stay at the posh hotel was done. I was, it was fair to say, distraught. No more bashful queuing for a fourth breakfast waffle. No more midday beers. No more public naps while the book I had been reading lay plonked across my face. When I had moved my belongings to a grotty, air-conditioner-less hovel on the other end of the beach, I had even begun to miss the foreign toddler who had taken to proudly urinating *into* the hotel pool instead of just in it, like all the other children.

To illustrate how far I had fallen: at no stage did the staff even bother to fold my towel into a swan, if you can bloody well believe that.

I suppose there comes a stage in any long journey where you grow weary of other travellers. For me, after Erena left, this became that day.

About the trip itself, I remained enthusiastic: I could not wait to make my way down the eastern coast and into the south. But other travellers – British couples and their delicate little stomachs, Germans and their obscenely peppy greetings, local machan types getting blackout drunk every night – these had all begun to grate. At the guesthouse, I began to be irritated by the profusion of unkempt beards and over-stuffed trekker backpacks around me. I myself had a trekking backpack and a scruffy beard. But I was way better than these people because I was me, and they, quite patently, were not.

Given my upset, it might have been best to avoid tourist congregations and yet I found myself at a beach restaurant that evening. Maybe mine was the kind of foul mood that demanded wallowing in; perhaps only once I had plumbed the depths of aggravation could I break through to the other side. So, there I sat, listening in on other travellers' conversations, almost daring myself to be further annoyed. It worked.

To begin with, the range of topics available for eavesdropping was almost too narrow to believe. Why is it that travellers talk to other travellers only about travel? I felt like I had heard some version of each of these conversations before. There were anecdotes about a close brush with death: 'In Nepal, my bus actually drove into a river, and I had to grab hold of a tree branch on the way down. It was so amazing. What happened to the other passengers? Yeah, they all drowned.' There were horror tales about third-world intransigence: 'You've got to be really careful when you're getting your visa renewed, you know. In Bangkok another woman had filled out her form with the wrong type of pen, and the guards threw her straight out of the seventh-floor window.' And, almost always, there was an account of an encounter with poverty: 'Mate – saw this one-armed kid picking food up off the street in Vietnam. Didn't have any food on me, you know, so I sawed one of my own arms off and gave him that.'

And please explain why certain breeds of millennial tourists are so dismissive about the nations they have been to. These people do not merely 'visit' or 'travel through' a place, they 'do' them, crossing off each nation as if each one will never be of use to them again. Did they not see the folly? As if in a three-week stay you could ever hope to experience even a fraction of what a country has to offer. One woman at a nearby table was a case in point: from what I could gather, she had spent just one week in Delhi and another in Maharashtra, but to hear her speak you'd think that the day she flew out, a nationwide alarm went off and 1.3 billion people immediately began demolishing their temples, burning history books, setting dynamite against the Himalayas, and throwing themselves into wells, the entire reason for India's existence fulfilled.

En route back to my guesthouse after the meal, more tourist shenanigans ensued. Two young Australian men stood by a rented scooter with a smashed headlight, warped front wheel, and a grazed front panel, the concrete wall nearby having been denuded of some of its blue paint.

'Aww mayte, waddya reckon?' one of them inquired, after I expressed a passing interest (like an idiot). 'D'ya think the owner'll notice?'

'Might catch this scratch on the fender.'

'Nah, she'll be right I reckon' he replied. 'Bit of a polish in the morning. That's all it needs.'

I left Trinco the next day. It had been good to me. Maybe too good. It had turned me into a pompous grump. I boarded a bus headed south in the morning and on the road passed houses with USAID or NEHRP painted on the roofs – homes built with foreign aid following the 2004 tsunami. More bone-dry fields glided by, populated by gaunt little goats and cows so skinny each of their ribs protruded. Dark women in colourful saris pottered around the kovil-adorned villages at first, sunlight glinting off their bangles and nose-studs. Later on, olive-coloured mosques, skullcaps, hijabs, and niqabs became commoner sights.

The journey felt not just like a return to reality but a reclaiming of myself. By the time I had disembarked in Batticaloa, a more cheerful frame of mind had returned.

On my first visit to Batticaloa, at the age of twenty-two, I had experienced one of the more pathetic moments of my life.

Perhaps I had been at a personal low ebb anyway. Nearing the end of my no-hope Arts degree, I had begged virtually every publication in the eastern hemisphere for a job and though to my delight I had landed a temporary gig covering a West Indies cricket tour of Sri Lanka, that tour was cancelled halfway due to a persistent monsoon, and I was left out of pocket and with a few empty weeks to fill. Knowing this, an uncle offered to take me on a trip out to Batticaloa, where he had just begun a scuba-diving operation. On one of the evenings he was busy. I was left to dine at a waterfront restaurant, alone.

I remember noticing early on, the happy faces all around me. Young parents sat with their joyful tots enjoying a meal in the open air, moonlight twinkling off the city's lagoon. Couples canoodled in the corners, lost in personal galaxies of infatuation.

And I recall not minding the music at first. A three-man acoustic band ambled from table to table, reeling off renditions of ancient English-language hits – Tom Jones, Cliff Richard, Lionel Richie, and the like. But, as my meal arrived, I was gripped by the dreadful thought that eventually the band may come and play to me. Suddenly, I felt exposed. Nothing terrified me more at this point in my life than the thought of being serenaded in the midst of a packed restaurant.

Soon enough, the moment came. Having played to every other table, they pointed their pot bellies in my direction and waddled over, perhaps out of some sense of not wanting to exclude me. Every atom in my being screamed at me to decline their advance, to tell them, 'No thanks, maybe next time.' My lips, however, formed only a weak smile, which was taken as encouragement. They played Engelbert Humperdinck's 'You're just too good to be true', of all things – a song I have never since heard without wanting to immediately leap into a vat of acid. When, halfway through the second chorus, one of the drummer's buttons popped open and his belly button began to flub with the rhythm inches from my face, the evening hit its true nadir. For the rest of my life, I will carry with me this memory: being ringed by three resplendently modest musicians, singing an English love song, while I – all alone in an enchanting setting – tried not to weep into my fried rice.

Traumatized though I was by that evening, the town itself was an infinitely hardier organism, having borne so much worse over the past few decades. Not only did Batticaloa find itself warred over, the 2004 tsunami had wiped entire neighbourhoods out, the water striking here with particular ferocity and in three distinct waves. In the Navalady stretch of sand – Batticaloa's eastern frontier – only members of ninety families were left alive where 260 had once lived. Many of those that survived had managed to cling to a palm tree or been carried out into the shallower parts of the lagoon. 'My God, I can't think about that day without feeling scared,' said Ranjan – a trishaw driver – to me, in broken Sinhala. 'I went back to find my house and I couldn't find my way even. The road, the trees, the buildings, everything had been washed off. Everything.'

How Batticaloa's town centre rebounded so emphatically, I may never quite wrap my head around. Where on that 2010 trip it had been a jumble of construction sites – roads being laid here, two-storey stores going up there, petrol sheds being expanded around the corner, and new bridges being built on the edges of town – it stood proud and shimmering now, cleaner than most urban centres in the country: its mid-town wriggling with columns of motorcycle traffic, its restaurants brimming with patrons, and its pavements trod by the smartly-dressed. Even at this late stage of the dry season, which had instilled a listlessness in so many other towns, Batticaloa thrummed with purpose. A tight space between two buildings on one of the main drags was being filled by a gazebo, where a local charity would hold a fund-raising sale the next day. A church near the centre of town had covered its surrounds with colourful bunting in anticipation of a coming celebration.

It was also with a quiet awe, that evening, that I beheld Batticaloa's spruced up public spaces – the likes of which many prominent Sri Lankan cities had either neglected or neglected to build altogether. At the edges of well-tended children's playgrounds with bright swing-sets and slides sat rows of parents on benches, overlooking one or another of the area's marshy lagoons. At the paved Mahatma Gandhi park on Pulliyanthivu – essentially a large, inland island, connected by three bridges to the mainland – I found myself in the company of couples watching the sun sink into the horizon.

On that first evening, the town seemed a small triumph – a place that had withstood repeated waves of disaster and set about the business of blooming the moment its siege had ended. Foreign aid following the tsunami had helped, but there was homegrown drive here too. At least part of the city's relative prosperity, locals testified, the area owed to its Muslims.

They were only Sri Lanka's third-largest ethnic group and never comprised more than one tenth of the population. Yet, Muslims have been instrumental to the island's economy for over a millennium.

Of the many blessings Mother Nature has bequeathed upon the island, none was more profitable to ancient Sri Lanka than its particular postcode in the Indian Ocean. Plonked at a maritime midpoint between east and west Asia, Sri Lanka also possessed such deep, inviting harbours, such warm, hospitable cities, and so much glinting produce of its own, it was almost as if the island's sole purpose on the planet was to be this roaring conflux of commerce. Silk sailed in from China, cargoes of spice from India, precious metals from Persia, and on the island did merchants meet to trade, distribute, and purchase goods for the return journey. When they departed, Sri Lankan kings waved each merchant vessel a fond goodbye while patting a fattened purse with the other hand – their trade levy having done its quiet work. Locals had their rubies and fragrant woods carried off to markets they had never heard of to be sold on to people whose lives they could scarcely imagine.

There were internal wars, of course, but in between had been the long, prosperous stretches that built the great monasteries of Anuradhapura and the hydraulic systems of the north-central plains. So pleasant does this era of the island's history seem, that modern Sri Lanka cannot help but romanticize it.

Chief among the sailors who facilitated Sri Lanka's success in medieval times were Arabs, known locally as Marrakkalayo – from the Tamil *maran* for wood, and *kala* for vessel. They had been purely itinerant at first, cruising in, trading, and departing. Sometime between the seventh and ninth century, they saw benefit in setting up more permanent bases on the island. Establishing in Sri Lanka a network of agents and sub-agents, they found they could streamline the sourcing of local merchandise for west Asian markets.

The first significant Muslim town on the island may have been in the southwest, at Beruwala, not far from the gem mines. By the high middle ages, several other Muslim settlements had sprung up around the coast. Alexander Johnstone, a chief justice of early-British Sri Lanka, gleaned the following from a medieval Cufic inscription he discovered near Colombo:

> Although the Mohammedan traders who were settled on Ceylon had acquired a great wealth and influence very early in the eleventh century ... it was during the twelfth and thirteenth centuries that they attained the highest degree of their commercial prosperity and political influence of that island. During that period, the great Mohammedan merchants of Mannar and Mantota received into the immense warehouses which they had established ... the most valuable produce of the island from their subordinate agents, who resided at the different sea-ports.... From their agents at Trincomalee they received rice and indigo; from those at Jaffna, the chaya root [or red dye], the wood of the black palmyrah tree, and the sea-shells called chanks; from those at Kudiramalai, pearls; from those at Puttalama areca nut, ebony, satin and calamander wood for furniture; from those at Colombo, cinnamon and precious stones; and from those at Beruwala, coconut oil and coir; and from those at Galle, ivory and elephants.

The Muslim traders' business went largely unimpeded, partly because they established strong links with the island's indigenous races. Their wives were local women who had converted to Islam (Arab women were typically not allowed to make the voyage). At some point, they ditched their native Arabic and adopted Tamil, which was the trading language of the region.

With Sinhala kingdoms, Muslim associations became especially cordial; a near-perfect symbiosis taking root. The Sinhalese, restricted by caste occupations and with little aptitude for maritime adventure, depended on the Muslims for access to foreign markets. Muslims, owning little land and having no customary occupations save as salespeople, leaned on the indigenous artisans for their supply. So highly valued, in fact, was Muslim seafaring skill and networking, that Sinhala kings took to deploying Muslims as trade envoys. In the thirteenth century, a merchant named Al-Haj-Abu-Uthman was dispatched to the Mamluk court of Egypt. Later, Kandyan monarchs employed Muslim diplomats to such an extent some Muslim families in the region still bear the Sinhala name Tanapatilagegedara (literally: 'of the ambassador's house').

Their faith also rarely came under threat because there was little animosity about how Islam came to be in Sri Lanka – its profile having been that of a peaceful, merchant people. Notably tolerant, also, were the strains of Buddhism and Hinduism that had taken root here. Concord settled for more or less a thousand years.

But then, eventually, the colonizers arrived and the bonhomie was ended. Not, immediately perhaps. Portuguese and Dutch harassment of Muslims on the seaboard drove many Muslims inland, where they were embraced and absorbed into the particular structures of the Kandyan kingdom. But the British, cleverer than their predecessors, saw benefit in mobilizing Muslims for their own ends. 'The good relationship that had prevailed,' writes historian Lorna Devaraja, 'deteriorated into one of competition, suspicion and ill will – the result of the policy of divide and rule and communal politics, which the British initiated from 1796 onwards.' As early as 1818 – during the Keppetipola rebellion – British officers reported some Muslims to be completely in their confidence. Race relations would continue to sour until in 1915, nationwide anti-Muslim riots erupted.

The tragedy, as ever, was this: what became bad under the British became worse when they left. In the past forty years, Sri Lanka's Muslims have found themselves besieged on two fronts.

It is a pity so many Sri Lankans choose to dwell on the quibbles that divide the nation, rather than the struggles that are common to us all. Frankly, there is much of the second sort. No matter where you are on the island, for example, no matter what your race or religion, you have, at some point in life, had to dive headlong into the nearest bush, pothole, or drain because, suddenly, a trishaw had mounted the pavement and begun approaching you at a speed that would see it leap clear over the nearest intersection, if only it could use your face for a ramp.

Not all trishaw drivers are so wired; I had met many kind and sensible purveyors of three-wheeled transportation on this trip. But a good percentage do have a madness about them and this sort was sprinkled equally across the island. There is also a profound nationwide resemblance in the manner many do business. Of this I was reminded the next morning.

Wanting to visit a mosque that had been infamously attacked twenty-six years ago, I hailed a trishaw near my guesthouse the next morning and asked the driver if he knew it. He spoke little English or Sinhala, but so confident was his smile and so assured the wobble of his head that I boarded straightaway. Eventually, I would come to realize that the driver had no idea where I wished to go. This was a widespread problem.

Rare, sadly, is the trishaw driver who will admit to a passenger that he does not know the way. Provide the name of any neighbourhood in the world – of a suburb in Pyongyang, say – and the driver will announce he knows the place, absolutely, that he was there just last week, and oh, his uncle also lives on one of the bylanes – the point being that you agree immediately to the hire. Once you are aboard he will set out in a completely random direction of his choosing, still with supreme confidence, still firmly committed to the charade. At no stage is any admission of ignorance made. If you were to tell him that he should really be going in the opposite direction, for instance, he would only click his tongue, swing his trishaw around so dramatically that cars have piled into each other in three different lanes, and then grumble, 'Ah, you want to take *that* route.' The implication here is that we could have all got there so much faster if only you had had the sense not to intervene.

Unfortunately, I was as clueless as the driver on this occasion, so we toured three different mosques before eventually we landed up at the right one. We were now in Kattankudy, five kilometres south of the centre of Batticaloa. Warm gusts blew through the narrow avenue, heat haze emanating from the cement paving. In the near distance, the bright pink of a bougainvillea tumbled out over a garden wall. Young men in topis glided by on bicycles.

The mosque – the Meera Jumma Masjid – rose to my right, two storeys tall and toffee-coloured; the three main entrances to its long body flung open. As I walked through the outer gate, a caretaker sweeping the steps looked up. Unbothered, he returned to his work. I ditched my flip flops and entered. Inside, rows of ceiling fans spun lazy circles and the polished red floor was cool beneath my feet. I had the mosque to myself.

It is the front wall, where the *mihrab* stands, that immediately drew my gaze. It was unsettling. Left untreated since the horrific evening of 3 August 1990, grey lacerations wrought by gunfire span the wall's breadth and blemish the nearby pillars. The building had clearly had renovations since. But the great cruelty it had endured, this mosque wanted to remember.

Survivors recall that Friday night having been especially sweltering. It had also very nearly been pitch-black, with the power to Kattankudy having been cut for weeks as a result of the fighting. Scores of men and boys had made their way to the many places of worship, just as they had done for generations, on Friday night. They had been in the midst of their Ishah prayer when gunfire was heard and squads of LTTE fighters stormed four mosques, shooting them up, flinging grenades, and disappearing back into the darkness, leaving a staggering 147 dead. The Meera Jumma alone lost seventy-eight of its faithful. Outside, a black plaque bore the names of the 'Shuhadas', or martyrs. The youngest victims – two brothers

– were aged six and eight. They had been at the nearby Husseiniya mosque, whose dead were also memorialized here.

Walking around the Meera Jumma, I found myself suddenly chilled by visions of that evening. From which direction had the Tigers come? How had the victims responded? There is no way they could have known the Tigers would strike with such ruthlessness but perhaps they had expected some sort of trouble – the Muslim community's relationship with the Tigers having frayed in the preceding months.

The Muslims' crime, as their attackers had seen it, was to have remained indifferent to the LTTE's struggle against the Sinhalese. In the eighties the Tigers had attempted to recruit Muslims, arguing their shared language equated to kinship and suggesting Muslims would only ever know true security in an independent Tamil state. But no more than a few handfuls of Muslims were ever won over – their timeworn impulse to preserve peace with the major races holding firm. All of a sudden, in 1990, the Tigers' patience snapped. No longer were Muslims to be courted. An all-out offensive would be waged instead. Muslims would find themselves driven from their homes and villages in the north or brutalized, as here. The week after the Kattankudy attacks, Eravur, a town to the north of Batticaloa, would suffer a near-identical tragedy.

Exiting the Meera Jummah, I walked the streets that enclosed the mosque, searching for someone who might fill me in on the attack's legacy. I stopped passersby and asked them if there was a mullah or an imam in the vicinity. I yelled over walls if I saw someone in their garden. I made myself a nuisance and received disinterested shrugs, or vague gesturing into the distance.

Eventually, I was taken pity on and an old man led me to the home of Mohammad Zubair, who lived on one of the lanes that ran parallel with the mosque. Zubair was tall and burly, with a lush prism of white hair protruding from his chin and a gleaming white T-shirt stretched thin over a pot belly. He had been reading a newspaper in his verandah when I found him.

'Where are you from?' he asked in accented Sinhala, unlatching his gate after I introduced myself.

'Dehiwala.'

'Ah, I have a friend there,' he said. 'Come, come. Come in and sit.'

Zubair, who gave off an aura of contentment, was generous with his time, yet intolerant of idle chat. Twice, he stopped my small talk dead: 'Yes, the dry season has been hard, but what are you really here for?' I worried this meant he would be guarded and businesslike in conversation, but he was in fact open and honest. His daughter brought coffee into the olive-green living room. Zubair's responses to my questions were detailed and considered.

'Of course our community still remembers what happened that night – that we can never forget'. He sat back in his chair, upright – relaxed, but serious. 'Every now and then, someone will still come and say, 'My son would have been forty-two today. He would have had his own family by now.' Everyone of that generation, whether they were in the mosque or not, will take that grief to their deaths. The wounds are too deep. There is no question about that.'

Zubair had been born in Kattankudy and had lived much of his life here, but on the night of the attack, had been overseas. He was, however, closely acquainted with the neighbourhood's attempts to heal in the decades since. The longtime president of the Meera Jumma's board, Zubair had his finger on the pulse of his neighbourhood, perceiving its trends and appetites, its fractures and faults.

'Anger … well, of course there was anger,' he said. 'There is anger still. They had had debates in the days after the attack and for a long time we had debates every week. You can't suffer a tragedy like that and not wish to fight back.'

A backlash from Kattankudy's Muslims certainly would have been unsurprising. Retaliation was, after all, the tragic rhythm of the war's first decade: one community unleashing violence upon another, then that group savagely recoiling, until soon all were roiled within this brutal, escalating vortex.

It is possible that the Tigers had even hoped to provoke the Muslims to violence. The worldview they wished to impose upon the island's Tamils was one of intractable victimhood. If widespread Muslim-on-Tamil riots had occurred, they may have succeeded in depicting their own race as evermore endangered – now not only by the chauvinist Sinhalese but by those 'shifty' coastal Muslims as well.

Yet a millennium of trade and business in Sri Lanka had perhaps hardcoded in the Muslims a cold pragmatism. Bloodshed was not their response.

'What can we really do, you know? We are a minority among minorities. A lot of our people were living in Tamil areas and Tiger-controlled places so if we started fighting, there would be no end.' I got the feeling Zubair had made this argument before, perhaps to members of his own congregation.

'The best thing, actually, was to break down the walls we had built with the other races. See, for generations, our sons had grown up just to go into the father's business. But that means we were quite closed off, isn't it? After the attacks we told our sons: go to school. Go and learn. Become a doctor. Become an engineer. Have contact with everyone around you. Get more Sinhalese and Tamil friends. When I grew up, if their father ran a textile shop, the sons also would do that, almost without fail. Now, since 1990, that all has changed. Only if the other professions don't work out do our children come back to the family shop.'

Zubair's own son was an electrician, who had worked in Batticaloa at first, before more lucrative work came up for him in Saudi Arabia. The white T-shirt Zubair wore, which I now noticed had a 'Saudi Aramco' logo on the left breast – had been a gift from him.

We chatted on – him occasionally inquiring about my travels and my own family, while I asked him more about how his community had changed. 'We also realized we have to live without showing off,' he said at one point. 'Even if some of us get wealthy, better to lead simple lives, no? Better to not arouse that kind of resentment.'

Eventually, we came to the subject of Sri Lankan Muslims' more recent plight. Though when the war finished Muslims should have been able to collect themselves – to unclench their muscles and exhale their fear – they have found themselves victims again, this time of violence breaking out from the south. The years between 2012 and 2014 had seen the rise of a fresh brand of Sinhalese nationalism, taking aim, this time, at Islam. In shrill, earsplitting speeches, the heavy-set, bespectacled monk, Gnanasara Thero – the figurehead of the movement – saw in the island's Muslims a vital enemy to Sinhalese Buddhism. 'The Sinhala-Bauddhaya will be gone in thirty years, if we let the Marakkalayo breed like this,' he had brayed, in a particularly hateful diatribe. 'The daughter, the mother, the grandmother, they are all giving birth in hospital at the same time.'

During those years, violence broke out in many neighbourhoods where for so many centuries Muslims and Sinhalese had peacefully coexisted. Every few months, a new rash of destruction ensued: Muslim shops were gutted, mosques were torched. Worst of all, in June 2014, full-scale riots erupted in the southwestern town of Aluthgama. A Sinhala mob charged through Muslim neighbourhoods, leaving four dead, eighty wounded, and innumerable homes and stores damaged beyond repair. The government at the time, led by Mahinda Rajapaksa, was accused of indifference to the situation at best and compliance at worst – Mahinda's brother and right-hand man, Gotabaya, having been seen in the company of Gnanasara. Arrests were slow and sentences lenient. The police and army personnel that had been deployed to becalm the violence had only stood by and watched, residents said.

'Look, here we have come to understand our situation is difficult,' Zubair said. 'Muslims in Sri Lanka are like the *dolki* drum – we get hit from both sides. Worst thing to do would be to retaliate by rioting back. But there are certain things we can do and we did that. We showed in the last election that even Sinhalese don't want these kinds of problems in our country.'

What in Zubair's mind his friendly swathes of Sinhalese had done, of course, was topple the Rajapaksas – first by voting in a more conciliatory and pluralistic government. Nationalist groups had briefly kept a lower profile since the transition of power, though at their core had remained still intact, snatching at every chance to agitate again.

'Yes, those extremists are still there, but there is a small freedom for us now,' Zubair said. 'Now we have the control of our lives, isn't it? We know that even if we can't use guns, we can still put a different kind of fight. Being in a democracy, we can get to the table – we can negotiate.'

This is not to say the Muslim community has been entirely blameless. For the remainder of our time together, we spoke of the rapid rise of Wahhabism – the most expansionary, restrictive, and fundamentalist of Islam's major sects in Sri Lanka. Where, in the 1990s, there was almost never a burqa or niqab to be seen on the street, face-coverings had burst into popularity in the twenty-first century, causing consternation in wider society – well beyond the nationalist mobs. Though Sri Lanka's traditional Sufi-influenced Sunni Muslims remained the overwhelming majority, the Sunnis had recently begun to feel imperilled by the velocity of the Wahhabi advance. Saudi clerics descended on towns such as Kattankudy by the busload. With a snap of their fingers, they acquired the funds to set up their own mosques and madrassas.

Eventually, Zubair had to leave for a meeting, and our

conversation drew to a close. 'We are always trying to correct other people's misunderstandings,' he said. 'People don't know that we are arguing with the Wahhabis as well.'

By the time I left his place, noon had come and gone. Later that afternoon, picking up my bags from the guesthouse, I boarded a bus heading south.

On my way out of Batticaloa, I couldn't help but be filled with a quiet admiration for Sri Lanka's Muslims. It was true their conciliatory approach to Sri Lankan life was dictated partly by fear: not only are they less populous than the major races, they are – geographically – thinly spread. But maybe there were lessons here yet. As Sri Lanka attempts this post-war reconciliation, as its people attempt to unstick the many daggers they had plunged in each other's bellies over decades, the nation could do worse than to take cues from the shrewd rationality of the Meeraj Jumma's congregants. Historically the island's most peaceful people, many Muslims had become fluent in the process of taking sober stock of their options, striking smooth compromises, and, vitally, moving on.

ELEVEN

A Rugged Corner

The first raptures of monsoon rain always come at dusk. As the sun sets, heavy clouds converge from all directions, like vendors on market day. Setting themselves up in the twilight, they lavishly and rambunctiously unload their goods.

In the previous week, there had been distant peals of thunder but no rain, the storms teasing the coasts without quite coming ashore. Finally, that evening, they made landfall. As my bus cruised southward along the coast, blinding forks of lightning zapped the earth, thunder drowned out the driver's bopping baila playlist, and droves of eastern folks were seen clumped beneath noisy *takaran* awnings in the towns.

It was the first proper deluge of my journey and the dramatic beginning-of-the-end for a dry season that had now officially been classified a drought. Soon, it was hoped, the squalls would invade the heartland and leave reservoirs across the nation replenished, cultivation land rejuvenated, and rivers coursing fat, muddy, and strong. With any luck, the rains would not overcompensate for their late arrival by dumping more water on the island than its rivers could flush out. Earlier in the year, the southwestern monsoon – which comes in May from the opposite direction – had precipitated a rash of floods and landslides that left well over a hundred dead and more than 200,000 displaced. Political transitions are tough enough, but the transformation of the global climate may become the greatest of Sri Lanka's challenges in coming decades. Already, each of the island's seasons has become more pronounced: the droughts now harsher than ever; each spell of downpours as intense as any in living memory.

Though the region would be grateful for the rain, my own journey was slightly complicated by it because the bus I was on would terminate at Akaraipattu and there was no guarantee there would be another one to take me fifty further kilometres to my next lodgings at Arugam Bay. When I disembarked at about 8 pm, the worst of the storm had ceased but a steady drizzle persisted.

I waited by Akaraipattu's roadside, steadily growing damper. An hour later, the second bus had not come. Cursing myself for having idled away too much of the afternoon in Batticaloa, I searched the vicinity of the bus halt, found another traveller who needed to get almost as far south as me, and convinced him to pitch in together for a long trishaw ride. He was an employee of the national electricity board who was currently stationed in Trinco and was headed home to visit his parents. 'Machan, you wouldn't believe how much land near home has gone up because of tourism, ah,' he grinned, while our trishaw puttered along one of the remotest coastal stretches on the island. Farmland, a noisy ocean, and lagoons slipped by. 'I bought a half-acre for 45,000 rupees twelve years ago. Now I won't sell it for less than twenty lakhs.'

We dropped him off and I went the few further kilometres to a hostel at Arugam Bay. The last of the evening's revellers were stumbling back to their lodgings along the sides of the main road.

The journey had been wetter, more expensive, and took longer than I imagined. But when, out of the next day, one of the more pleasant surprises of the trip would tumble out, it would turn out to have been worthwhile.

The southeast is my favourite corner of Sri Lanka. Maybe that is why I saved it for so late in the trip. It is a wild place. Four major national parks are located here and in them all manner of untamed delights: fearsome tuskers, four-metre crocodiles, irascible sloth bears, vast herds of wild water buffalo, flocks of water fowl, and the sleek, shadowy, princes of the Sri Lanka jungle – leopards, whose status as apex predators has seen them grow bigger and more powerful here than in most forests of the planet.

Perhaps it is because the region was out of bounds during parts of my childhood that it has always seemed so bewitching. Not only were long trips in those days complicated by busted roads and endless military checkpoints, these parks had actually been caught up in the violence – the LTTE having controlled the area at the height of their powers. Locals from nearby villages remember years of being ruled by fear. 'Every evening, for months, we used to leave our house and creep into the jungle to spend the night,' one woman from a nearby village told me. 'At least with animals you can do something no? You can put kerosene on the ground for snakes or wave a branch and chase away a leopard. If a person with a gun breaks down your door and comes to kill you, then what? If they come, nothing to do.'

Arugam Bay itself, meanwhile, had recently become a thriving tourist town, though I must admit I did not pay it much attention on this visit. Look, there are stunning stretches of palm-lined sand, a good left-hand break if you are a surfer, beach bars to drink yourself silly at, and tall dunes to frolic on. But having so recently been to Trincomalee I was temporarily unenamoured of beaches and the holidaymakers who visited them. The only reason I was even staying in this town was because it had an abundance of low-cost accommodation and my budget was nearly exhausted. I shared a dormitory that night with two snoring Dutchmen, ate a breakfast of coconut roti and lunu miris, and, by late morning, was heading even further south to the first of those national parks – Kumana – on a scooter I had hired.

The previous night's rain did not appear to have come this far down the coast. Here, the rice and onion fields remained shriveled, the ancient reservoirs were as depleted as anywhere, and, as I sped along the tarmac, the heat seemed to reach down through my airways to harass even my lungs for their moisture. Where the farmlands of the north and east were generally paper-flat, there was a ruggedness to this landscape – giant boulders laying stubbornly amidst paddies and outcrops of grey granite hulking above the desiccation. When I got to the town of Paanama, the road to Kumana turned inland into thicker greenery. It was evenly paved for the first few hundred metres but soon gave out to gravel and eventually became a bumpy dirt track. I cannot say I navigated it with much grace. This was because suddenly, I found myself alone on a forest road strewn with elephant dung.

No variety of faeces could ever be as intimidating. Of that I am convinced. I mean, here is an animal whose one turd can be as large as a human head, which can jettison more refuse in a single shitting than can be contained in a wheelbarrow, and whose insides are so industrious that, depending on the part of the world, elephants are either cursed for stripping entire forests bare, or lauded for dispersing a jungle's worth of seeds by way of their collective anii.

Some of the dung along this road was withered and crusty. Other specimens lay in neat little pyramids, like cannonballs awaiting launch at an enemy frigate. But the worst – the ones that really filled me with dread – were the damp, fresh piles, whose pungence prompted the shuddering thought that I would encounter its ejector around the next corner. My mind began to run through all the terrifying elephant stories I had come across on the trip: the journalist who had his head trod on in Minneriya; the old woman who was trampled in Polonnaruwa; the tale of an older man near Ritigala who had emitted bloodcurdling death screams as he was bashed around by a tusker. As the dirt track began to venture through thick jungle, every tree trunk began to resemble an elephant leg.

Oh god, is that a tusk? No, just a tree branch.

Swaying branches became moving tusks. A few times, I was convinced I heard ominous crunching of twigs nearby, only to soon realise it was only my wimpy 50 cc motorbike riding over loose rocks. I spooked myself at virtually every turn and veered manically all over road. It was an eighteen-kilometre journey of unbridled cowardice.

I did encounter elephants that day but thankfully this was in the relative safety of the safari jeep I had hired when eventually I reached the entrance to the park. By then the sun had already sapped the day's energy. My driver, a wisp of a fellow, spoke slowly and drove even slower, pausing often to stare wordlessly into a thicket for a minutes before reapplying a gentle sole to the accelerator. The animals were also semi-somnolent. Almost absent-mindedly did the elephants – a herd of around six –

forage by the roadside. 'You've come at the wrong time of day to see active wildlife,' the driver muttered, after we had set off again and spotted nothing in the bush for many kilometres. 'They are all hiding in the jungle now.'

He was right of course. Most animals are only glimpsed at dawn and dusk. And yet, the safari would soon find a way to become emphatically redeemed. Though it was the ibises, pelicans, and herons who first took my attention when we came across a vast sweep of wetlands, I soon spied something else in the distance: a copse of coconut trees rising up above the surrounding canopy. I was perplexed. I had never seen coconuts this deep in a national park before. How is it that a village crop came to be set so incongruously, and in such a neat little grove, here?

My driver did not know but a wildlife official at a nearby lookout had the answer. 'That's the old Kumana village,' he said. 'You can still see parts of the old buildings where the people used to live.'

'Used to live?' I asked. 'What happened?'

'They were evacuated by the army in the early 1990s, I think. During the war. Military couldn't protect them here.'

'They must have been like Veddahs no?' Veddahs were indigenous folk, some of whom still lived as hunter-gatherers in various forests.

'No, no. Definitely not. Not Veddahs. The people here were quite developed and well-educated. There was even a school there.'

'So why were they here, so far from everything?'

'Far as I know, they were descendants of a group that ran away from the 1818 rebellion.'

'The Keppetipola rebellion? In Uva?'

'That's the one. These people followed the Kumbukkan Oya river down from the upcountry and came all the way down. Lived off the jungle mostly, I think.'

I was stunned. This, I had to see. In my time in the hill country, I had heard of folks who fled the devastation wrought by the British but never imagined communities had been displaced quite this far, to this fearsomely rugged corner of the island.

Turning left at the edge of the marsh, we bounced along a skinny track and, soon, the branches parted and the old schoolhouse hove into view. Something, however, was amiss. This did not have the look of a building that had been abandoned for more than two decades. In fact, the main classroom had surely had its roof re-tiled in the last few years and its low walls whitewashed even more recently. The jungle, also, had been neatly trimmed back. We left the jeep, entered the building, and soon discovered who was responsible for the upkeep. 'Sri Lanka Sinha Regiment, 23rd Army Corps', read the blue-and-pink chalk writing on the blackboard. Graffiti, in Tamil as well as Sinhala, marked the surrounding walls. Bullet-holes in the plaster had been patched up.

Only the schoolhouse had been resurrected, however. The remainder of Kumana village had been left to endure the ravages of the jungle – a relic now, strewn with overgrown bases of clay structures that might once have been homes; weathered rocks that looked like tombstones; and the coconut grove itself. The Kumbukkan Oya, bordered by the enormous kumbuk trees that gave the river its name, coursed about a hundred metres away. Just beyond that, out of sight, roared the Indian Ocean.

Here, it was clear, had been a settlement of refugees: folks so aggrieved by British violence, they escaped into wilderness, settling only when they literally ran out of land. The jungle, for them, was not a place of peril but of protection.

Animals they could chase away, they may have reasoned. But men with guns? If they came, nothing to do.

I tracked down a former resident of Kumana village that afternoon. Having made inquiries at a large temple following another fretful ride back to Paanama, I was directed to a hamlet approached by a sandy track. It was separated from the ocean only by vast, grassy dunes.

Raamal Appu Dhanapala grinned at the mere mention of his old village. He was a wiry man to whom a full head of greying hair remained but whose front teeth had absconded. Springing to life as if he had waited years for this day – for a stranger with a notepad to turn up on his verandah – he had, within minutes, offered me a plate of the rice-and-fish-curry lunch he was eating, found a second chair, moved us both out to beneath the shade of a fledgling mango tree, and begun to pour forth. His account of Kumana was impossibly idyllic.

'Puh, what danger?' he snapped. 'The jungle animals would never, ever hurt us. Even these people in Paanama think that our lives were so very risky those days. Couldn't be more wrong. No one got bitten by a snake even. We were part of the jungle, and the jungle was part of us. That was all the protection we needed.'

Laced with enchanting embellishments was his portrait of Kumana. The village had been a Sinhala-Buddhist outpost but Tamils had married in to it, he insisted. ('No race problems in Kumana: only human kindness.') About forty families had resided there and their crops always prospered, he professed.

'Actually, you should have seen how we ate then – like royals.' He seemed almost offended when I asked if they had been subsistence farmers. 'Jungle fruit as big as my hand, yams as long as my forearm, coconuts, buffalo curd, and wild honey every day. None of these poisonous preservatives. You should have seen.'

He believed so emphatically in every word, I was tempted to buy his stories myself. It almost seemed conceivable that the ox-cart that supplied the village store was often sent back fuller than it arrived – the forest supposedly having produced such a vast bounty. The baskets full of wriggling river fish he said they netted every day, I could almost bring to mind.

'People ask: 'How did you manage to live in a place where it takes two days to get to the hospital?' I tell them we didn't need the hospital. We had the goodness of the land in our bodies. Our children were so healthy and strong. Out here people think this is the good life, but you should have seen our village those days. Even anyone who visited never wanted to leave.'

And then, without warning, Dhanapala became solemn.

His boasts, which had brought the garden alive, suddenly gave out. 'But, you know, we all did leave.' He sat back in his chair, right hand idle on his plate, and sighed. 'We left the life we had built and the land our ancestors had passed on to us. The army came. We were told we had to go.'

The evacuation had occurred in stages, between 1990 and 1992. The fighting, by that time, had grown heavy in the eastern reaches of the island and the army had said they could do without having to protect such a far-flung inhabitation. Thus, a community made by one war found itself forcibly dissolved by another.

'There is no one in our village who didn't go with a heavy heart. Some people had to be threatened even.'

'But you were at least given land to resettle, weren't you?' I ventured.

'Yes, but what kind of land? This sandy soil only. Tell me, what can you grow here? Some people in the village were given plots near upcountry areas, but even they are complaining. I'll tell you: nothing can ever be like the earth you grew up on, isn't it?'

He was silent for a moment. When next he spoke, a little anger had bubbled up.

'They say they kicked us out only for our own protection, but can we really accept that? If that is the case, why was our village not given back after the war? It has been seven years now. Just imagine: this was a place that our ancestors had lived in for 170 years. Did the military really want to keep us safe, or did they want to rob us of our land?'

His was a grievance voiced often, but largely from the

tens of thousands of Tamils and Muslims who had been displaced in the north and east. Only for a miniscule fraction of the southern population did it apply but the complaint, nevertheless, was almost identical.

When we had finished our plates, Dhanapala had talked himself to near exhaustion. He would soon disappear indoors. Not long after, I would ride back to Arugam Bay. But before we parted, the old man left me with two treasures: a pair of *kavi* – or lyric poems – he had crafted during his twenty-seven years of exile. Having dictated them, he insisted I read each one back and rebuked me for every misheard syllable. At his request, the more beautiful of these is reproduced below:

Nil wal kale avidina vita sathuta danei
Kumbukkan ganga diya naavama suvaya anei
Kalaa rodhaka ipadunu mata duka nodanei
Mawbima mage kalabala mada ahimi vunei

So much of the *kaviya*'s artistry I have sadly failed to capture. Nevertheless, here is my best translation:

My heart would stir to raptures to walk in that vibrant wood,
Refreshed in the Kumbukkan's waters; the river did me good,
No woe in my strap of jungle, no sorrow since my birth,
And then in war and trouble, I lost my native earth.

You may fail to set your alarm in Sri Lanka but never fret: the nation will thoughtfully conjure up some early-morning cacophony to pluck you brusquely from your dreams. In Dehiwala, a *choon paan* mobile bakery plays monotone jingles from its loudspeaker at dawn, sending me cursing bleary-eyed into bedroom furniture. Villages in the southern province are roused by the rackety croaks of peafowl. In the north, Tamil pop music seems to be the daybreak weapon of choice. If none of the above are forthcoming, the high-decibel holiness of various places of worship will step gallantly up to do the job. On this journey, however, nothing woke me as consistently as the early-morning throat-cleansing opera that many Sri Lankans perform as part of their daily ablutions.

It is a strange routine. Most young folk would not be caught dead purging their airways like this. Yet, when a Sri Lankan's strength has waned and weariness has entered the body, enmities against old friends or extended relatives are put aside and total war on phlegm is declared instead. My Sinhala grandfather had been a particularly noisy throat-cleaner, charging his lungs with great, audible inhalations before bringing great globules up in ferocious hacking fits. If there were several elderly people in a neighbourhood, a sort of shift-system appeared to emerge. One old man would begin the day's coughing before the old lady two houses away would pick up where he left off and so on, until soon, a long, spluttering chorus has seized the morning.

The caretaker of the hostel at Arugam Bay had been quietly spoken in our exchanges but, on my second morning there, it was to the sound of him dragging phlegm out of every last bronchiole that I awoke. The volume was almost impressive. I have also never worked out why older people make a point of rising at such indecent times.

Thanks to that early start, I was heading inland by mid-morning, then later turned south, having switched buses at the town of Monaragala. Both bus rides either skirted jungle, or – as with the second leg – cut right through it: the B35 from Monaragala to Tissamaharama bisecting Lunugamvehera National Park. It is on this stretch that one of Sri Lanka's more notorious highway bandits operates. A bull elephant has, over the course of a decade, taken to blocking off one lane of the road, compelling travelers to hand over fruit through an open window as they pass. Banana vendors have even set up in the vicinity to help cater to this singular market. See what I mean about the southeast being a wild place?

It was a wildness I revelled in over the next twenty-four hours. Having holed up in the town of Tissamaharama that night, I booked myself a seat on a safari jeep with a French family of four and a solo Japanese tourist. By dawn the next day we were riding into Yala – the most famous of the national parks in the region.

We saw little animal life in the first half of our safari but the ride was nevertheless enlivened by the patriarch of the French clan, who grew fantastically irritated with each near miss. If, for example, the passengers of a passing jeep reported a leopard sighting, our Frenchman would fly into a rage – chastising our driver for failing to show us the animal, then insisting we inspect the area though it was clear it had long since disappeared. After a few minutes of staring at boulders through his heavy-duty binoculars, his anger would reach a zenith – his long, nasal follicles and the imperilled hairs on his scalp quivering as one with fury. His wife and two teenaged children, meanwhile, looked as if they would like nothing more than to be let out of the jeep and left to the jungle's perils. Occasionally they would venture a soothing word, or a reassuring squeeze of his arm. This only sent him into greater fits of tremulation.

It was just before 9 am that our luck turned and spirits were lifted. A sloth bear was suddenly found foraging in a bush. Later, two leopards were seen kipping in a tree – fifty metres back from the road but visible through the binoculars. Also making an appearance were hordes of wild boar, rows of basking crocodiles, mongooses, eagles, water fowl, and a vine snake.

That afternoon, catching another bus to Hambantota, I visited a fourth national park – Boondala – which afforded sublime evening views over bird-filled wetlands, as well as glimpses of Olive Ridley turtles grazing below a clifftop lookout. Tourist beaches might grate after a while, but who could ever tire of this? When coming from the lower branches of a wild banyan tree, even the croaks of peafowl were not totally without charm.

And yet, for all its thrills, the park was not everything it pretended to be. Boondala is famed island-wide for its flamingoes, to the extent that they are the species most associated with the park. The birds, however, have not been here for over a decade. Way back in 2006, they had taken flight to their summer feeding grounds in Gujarat's Rann of Kutch, never to return. The exact reason for this exodus no one has quite been able to pin down, but leading theories suggest that the birds had run out of food. A recent irrigation project is understood to have altered a salinity of Boondala's wetlands, which in turn had decimated populations of the particular insect larvae flamingoes had fed on.

Even in this untamed corner of a wild island, here was a reminder that not all species will proliferate forever. Here was a reminder of the damage human intrusion can wreak.

Through much of my trip, I had stayed in low-cost rooms that occasionally veered towards squalor. Even by those standards my lodgings in Hambantota were grimy.

Having got in around noon the previous day (before the Boondala safari), I had wandered into a guesthouse that from the outside had looked pleasant enough – fruit trees skirting the front yard and palms peeking out from behind the roof. Inside, however, the room was a fiesta of dilapidation. The walls were festooned in mildew and peeling paint. The once-white curtains appeared to have been soaked in snot. Also, the windowsills had played host to a terrible insect genocide, the shower was a gecko-poo storage silo, and the bathroom mirror had been the canvas for a toothpaste-splatter painting.

Quite clearly, the room had not had a guest in weeks, and the next morning, the owner admitted as much. 'We're finding it very difficult these days, *malli*,' she told me. 'We built the place expecting Hambantota to develop. Now, since this nonsense new government has come in, we will soon be destitute.'

She had on a fat gold necklace and held a shiny Chinese smartphone, so perhaps she was not quite on the brink of starvation yet. But still, the crux of her contentions was coherent. The new government was unquestionably 'nonsense', as any Sri Lankan government tends to be. It had also overseen a sharp decline in the district's stock.

Only two years had passed, in fact, since Hambantota had been Sri Lanka's city of the future – the area still bedecked with recently-constructed amenities such as a lavish conference centre, a vast cargo port, a colossal cricket stadium, and, most impressive of all, a spanking international airport built to handle the largest commercial jets on the planet, along with one million passengers a year. All of this was joined by a network of perfect four-lane highways, the likes of which cannot be seen anywhere else on the island. How such resplendent infrastructure came to be built in a far-flung agricultural district with a population of roughly 600,000 will take some explaining, so stay with me.

The investments had been made by former president Mahinda Rajapakse (personal motto: making Sri Lanka wildly prosperous, one immediate family member at a time). Having found the nation in need of a second major commercial hub to ease the pressure on Colombo, he chose to sink borrowed Chinese money into this region, which is a key component of his political power base, because it is from this district that his family hails.

Well, that is about the size of it. I suppose it is not that difficult to explain.

Still, the plan to modernize what was essentially a string of fishing towns spaced amid wide swathes of jungle had begun to flounder *even while* Rajapakse held high office. The port – the one project that had had even a mild chance of success – could not attract the traffic the government banked on, despite its situation along the busiest shipping channel on the planet. Most airlines, meanwhile, saw no reason to fly to the southeast – their planes in danger of making mincemeat of migrating birds in any case.

When public criticism of this misuse of funds began to mount, the ruling family and its surrogates produced a number of excuses. Their vision for Hambantota could only be realized over the course of many decades, they argued, and should in no way be judged on its first two years of rollicking failure. The projects might have a chance of gaining some traction, they roared, if only the traitorous opposition party ever stopped poisoning public opinion. India's lack of support was soon blamed and, later, a Western conspiracy to undermine the project was contrived. Just when you thought herons and spoonbills would be berated for having so maliciously established centuries-old migration routes exactly where the planes were supposed to operate, Rajapakse was voted out. With no little pleasure, the new folks in charge abandoned Rajapakses' vision.

The morning after the Boondala safari, I ventured out to see the palatial Hambantota District Secretariat. It was the one monument to Rajapakse rule that still remained freely accessible to the public, with the port and conference centre out of bounds and the world's emptiest airport open only to its trickle of weekly passengers. The 35,000-capacity stadium had also been shut up and padlocked for over a year, though that particular bonfire of public funds I had been to many times before. It is perhaps the only sporting venue in the world where wildlife officials were deployed to prevent spectators from straying into the range of a nearby elephant herd. Elephants had also been known to bust the fence and wander on to the pitch in months when the ground went unused. All sorts of other mishaps have taken place in the vicinity. Once, two drunk men were seen fighting in the stands and news later spread that one had wound up murdering the other after they had been ejected from the venue. Another time, driving back to his lodgings after an evening game, a colleague had crashed into a resting water buffalo, killing the animal, writing off his car, and setting off a small stampede. Have I mentioned the southeast is wild?

But at the District Secretariat that morning, there was no wildlife, nor in fact, activity of any description. It was 10 am on a Wednesday – a time when every other government office in the country would be wriggling with file-wielding patrons, bristling queues pouring out most doorways. The Secretariat, however, was magnificent in its stillness. The main building rose four storeys tall, with a shiny gabled roof, and straw-coloured two-storey wings sprawling handsomely on either side. All of this enclosed a palm-lined courtyard fronted by a water fountain.

Inside, in the cavernous lobby, there was not so much as a surly security guard to shoo folks to another building, nor a dead-in-the-eyes government receptionist to spit vague directions. I climbed two storeys before I spied movement: a ceiling fan cooling a spectacularly empty room. When eventually I came across flesh-and-blood government staff, they were mostly making use of the lifetime pass to indolence that is a position in the Sri Lankan government. Two women in saris sat idly at desks in a room that could have comfortably accommodated twenty. Three men in shirts and slacks stood chit-chatting in another desolate hall. The whole building was like this: scores of unproductive bureaucrats spread between dozens and dozens of empty rooms – many of which had been closed up but others which had lights on and fans whirring for the benefit of nobody.

It was depressing. Many weeks ago, at the Grama Niladhari's office in Dehiwala, only the tip of Sri Lanka's ineffective state machinery was on view. On proud display here was government waste on an industrial scale. Many have labelled the Hambantota projects 'white elephants', after the Thai royal practice of presenting unpopular courtiers with tuskers that were ruinously expensive to maintain. Yet, with Sri Lanka now strangled by foreign debt, thanks in part to these developments, even that analogy seems insufficient. This is more like if your white elephant had also developed a gambling addiction and got in deep with loan sharks.

As I made my final sweep of the building, I spotted two rows of beautiful villas set some distance back from the Secretariat. There were about two dozen of them in total, each with a carport and perfectly manicured gardens. These were not homes for the tsunami-affected or the many rural poor but for government hotshots posted to the district. Rarely on this seven-week journey had I felt anger at my country. It began to overtake me now.

I suppose I had not expected to feel this way in the part of Sri Lanka I loved the most. I had arrived with memories of the many kindnesses I had known here on previous visits: of strangers who had shown me around their towns; of the policemen who had happily gone out of their way to provide a letter absolving me of fault in a motor accident; of shopkeepers who had turned up their fingers and smiled 'what to do?' when I had been short of change for the groceries they let me buy. How is it that such folks elect the kinds of fattened, egotistical, mass-manipulators they clearly do not deserve? How could they be so blindly complicit in their own screwing over?

Later, I came to realize how this swindle comes together. Whenever a new road is laid down, or a power grid bolstered, those in power ensure it is they who are personally associated with this improvement to life. They emblazon their names upon every public project, dominate the limelight in the blessing ceremony to inaugurate new infrastructure, and generally impress upon the people that it is they – not the government at large – that has delivered them this progress. They build houses for the underprivileged, hand out trishaws, tractors, and school uniforms, always insisting that they alone are the public's saviour. That any threat to their power is a threat to the people, whether those challenges arise from opposing politicians, or from the mere function of democracy itself.

I was still in a sour mood when I left Hambantota that afternoon. I picked up my bags from the guesthouse and boarded another bus. The refurbishment of the coastal road to the west had been another Rajapakse-era project. Not that it acquits the waste elsewhere but this one, at least, was of some use to the public.

TWELVE

Southern Venom, Southern Warmth

The government may move at a dopey pace, a busted landline might take months to fix, and you could spend long enough in a hospital queue to contract everyone else's diseases, but if there is one operation which Sri Lanka performs at breakneck velocity, it is the mass production and distribution of gossip.

What a wonder this is. People who in regular life are no more productive than sea cucumbers become enterprising and electric when in possession of tasty information. The victims, in turn, are stunned by the rate at which stories travel. Married women have shared brief conversations with men at their workplace and come home to find the entire neighbourhood aflame. Men who have offered female friends a ride home on their motorbikes, meanwhile, have found themselves aggressively maligned before the lady has even been dropped off.

And it is fear of this light-speed web of gossip that puts many couples on edge in public. The pair I shared the back seat with near Matara would nestle into each other when the bus was between stops, but the moment it slowed, hands were unclasped, necks were craned, and new passengers were inspected. If a neighbour or relative got wind of their unsanctioned romance, the yelling-at of a lifetime may result.

Thankfully, I never experienced this anxiety myself, but my parents report having been very nervous travelers through the early 1980s. They had more reason than most to be fearful. To begin with, my mother was from a devoutly Catholic background and my father from a Buddhist family. Worse: for the majority of their courtship, my father had also been a married man.

They assure me this was far less outrageous than it seems, though the story is not without a dash of scandal. My father's first marriage had been little more than a transaction to shore up his family's finances. The reason their accounts had been depleted in the first place, apparently, was because my grandfather – the career prison guard – had been suspended from work upon charges of taking bribes. Though he was eventually cleared, the years in which his case was heard were tough on the family. Little heed was paid to the reluctance of the son being married off to a wealthier clan. The payout was what mattered.

The one concession my father drew through the ordeal, however, was that he be allowed to settle into a career before he took up the union properly, and this – it turned out – would be the deal's undoing. No more than a month after my father's first marriage was registered, he met my mother and fell in love. Whatever obligation my father had to his legal wife, he abandoned. To this day, this is a woman he has not spent more than a few chaperoned minutes with.

My father remembers my Catholic grandmother having been suspicious of him from the outset. ('She took one look at me and decided she didn't like me'.) When his marital status was revealed, dislike became disgust and my mother – now lavishly rebuked at home – was goaded constantly to give up the affair.

There are excellent stories from this period. Once, when my mother had taken a half-day off work and a work colleague had relayed this information to my grandmother via the gossip web, my grandmother had shown up at the station platform while my parents sat inside a train, awaiting departure. Such was the fear she inspired, my father had sprung rapidly to his feet upon spotting her, blazed a trail through the cabin, and exited on to the tracks, unseen. Another time, my grandmother had made the three-hour trip from her house in Negombo to my father's home in Panadura, just to rain raucous abuse upon his family. Even now, my father's siblings speak of that day with a hushed dread. They had found out that day, as many had through the years, that they were dealing with an elemental force of a woman.

And yet, for all her objections, my grandmother had never opposed my parents' romance on the basis of race. On that front she was perfectly accepting. This is partly because although my mother's family are Tamil, they are from a particularly tolerant community – numbering around 12,000 – called the Barathas. Having arrived from South India between the sixteenth and eighteenth centuries, they had settled on the western coast and quickly set about establishing economic ties with the Sinhalese. In the last half century, this has progressed to widespread inter-marriage – many in our extended family having found spouses outside the community. I have also never met a Baratha who is less than fluent in Sinhala.

It was not their language but their traditional industry that played on my mind as I arrived in the south. While still in Tamil Nadu, the Barathas had dug out a niche as merchants who traded with fishers – usually selling fishing and boat supplies to those who went out to sea. A subset of the Paravar caste, it is likely earlier generations of Barathas had themselves been fishers and seafarers. It is these ancestors, I liked to think, who passed down to me my love of the ocean.

I stepped off the bus at Weligama quietly gleeful. A friend there had promised to arrange for me a boat trip. The next day, I would be returning to my roots. I would be reaching back through the centuries and connecting – in some small way – to my family's past.

Or so, at least, I thought.

'We leave at two in the morning,' Bomal told me. We had been introduced the evening I came to Weligama, while he was sat on his front steps, shirtless and swaying, a bottle of *gal* arrack by his feet. 'If you are not at the harbour by two, we will still leave. Can't help. We have to catch some bait before dawn.'

By 2:15 am there was no sign of Bomal as I stood on the road into the harbour. By 2:30, I had slumped down against a gate. By 2:45 I had fallen asleep. At around 3, I became vaguely aware of a stray dog preparing to relieve himself near me when a figure sprang suddenly out of the night and yanked me to my feet.

'Don't sleep here with the dogs, what is wrong with you?' He brushed cement dust off my shoulder. 'Ah … you're waiting for Bomal? Don't know if that idiot will come even. Come, come, come … let's drink a tea. I am also waiting for the fellows on my boat. Pricks who said we would leave at two. Still not here.'

My saviour was short and rotund, with thick, ropey forearms. He had on a chewed-up grey cap. Wisps of hair peeking out its sides were also grey. Having led me to the awning of his house across the road, he roused his poor, ancient mother, who had been asleep on the floor in the front room. When she brought us the tea in plastic cups, her narrow wrists shook.

'Always giving the wrong time, these pricks, never here, what to do?' I may have learned his name. At that hour, it had not stuck in the memory. 'You're from Colombo? You must be used to being on time. The ass who owns our boat is probably lying drunk on the road. Woman doesn't let him back in when he drinks. Big woman she is. Angry all the time. Get scared thinking of her, even. When she hits the children, whole village hears. *Dhadaang!* Come, come … finish your tea. Amma! AMMA! Come, will you? Take the cups.'

Soon, ambling groups of fishermen began to appear; sarongs hitched up to the knees, scruffy shirts unbuttoned to the sternum. 'Have you seen Bomal?' My companion would holler. They shrugged, drifting on towards the harbour.

When he did eventually appear, it was nearly half-past three. With Bomal were two others: my boat-mates for the day. I bade goodbye to the man who had taken me in and stood around uselessly at the beach as the three fishermen loaded two styrofoam containers into a long, narrow *oruwa* canoe. We rowed out to the middle of the harbour and transferred ourselves and the boxes to the big fishing boat. The anchor was hauled up, a diesel engine puttered us out of port, and Weligama's dim cluster of lights began to grow distant. Soon, the town had virtually disappeared.

It was not until later – after sunrise – that I could make out the details of our vessel. With a chipped sky-blue hull of fibreglass and a deck of slatted, greying wood, it was about thirty metres from stern to bow. The cabin to the rear was no larger than a standard bedroom closet. Inside were three sooty aluminum pots, a half-sack of rice, a single-burner gas stove, a biscuit tin filled with garlic, ginger, onion, chilli, and spices, a bag of sugar, and loose-leaf tea. The bamboo mast at the centre of the boat rose to about three metres. Tied to it, several fishing rods and volley-ball sized styrofoam buoys that rubbed squeakingly against each other. In plastic boxes at the front of the boat were nylon long-lines fitted with steel hooks dangling from short, secondary lines every three feet. These boxes would be accessed constantly – the long-lines bringing in virtually all of the day's yield.

Of the three men, Bomal was the most laidback, often lounging atop the cabin with his legs up on a tyre (an improvised lifesaver), humming contentedly to himself. Afflicted was he by each of Sri Lanka's working-class vices. In the early morning he had smelled still of arrack. From the moment we boarded, beedi cigarettes were produced from a cloth pouch. Once an hour, a fat wad of betel would be rolled up and chomped on. Such teeth that remained to his checkerboard grimace were stained a rusty orange.

Amare, the oldest man on board, wore a faded sarong over spindly legs, and he alone of us four was bareheaded. His first act had been to slice up the cuttlefish he had bought the previous evening, to bait a long-line with the pieces. Before dawn, he had worked quickly, throwing his line repeatedly overboard and reeling it in at the stern. That first cuttlefish was bait to catch more cuttlefish, which in turn would lure the bigger fish later in the day. He also worked as helmsman from a spot at the back of the boat where throttle and rudder could be simultaneously manipulated. A handheld GPS was his main navigational instrument.

The third crewman Shantha – a short, dark, broad-shouldered, boulder of a man – caught almost twice as much fish as anyone else. Not for him were diversions like smoking, chewing or chatting. When he took up his post on the stern at daybreak he was more-or-less rooted there till lunch – letting his line out over a fat and calloused index finger, pulling it back, re-baiting, then repeating the process every few minutes. Whenever he brought a fish over the gunwale, he would kiss it before flinging it on deck. Shantha worked as if in a trance; the muscles in his forearms rippling to an unheard rhythm.

So there we were in the deep blue, three lifelong fishermen and myself. Despite the very early start, I had boarded the vessel with confidence: I was sure this would be an idyllic maritime day. I would lend these men a hand with their labour, I thought, while they lent me an intimate glimpse into their profession, a manly bond forming throughout. Perhaps they would even remark on how quickly I took to their work – a compliment to which I would respond with an unassuming smile and a line about how fishing was in my blood, see, so it was only natural, and really it is my forebears that deserve all the credit.

This, sadly, was not how it panned out.

On the calmest, sunniest day any seafarer could hope for, I was a constant saboteur of their operation. I fumbled, I interfered, I botched, blundered, and ruined. The only wonder was that they did not truss me up and toss me overboard. Though in fact, at times during the day, I sort of wished they had.

It was while the men were still catching cuttlefish in the pre-dawn that my woes had begun. While the others worked the long-lines, Bomal had fetched a landing net with a circular rim about the circumference of a watermelon, attached to a two-metre bamboo pole. He would crouch by the edge of the boat in the low light and, just as the white outline of a cuttlefish neared the surface, send the rim skimming across the water, flicking his wrists to snare the fish. Over the course of five minutes, he made six sweeping splashes and missed only twice. I was not alone in gawking with admiration. 'I've never seen anyone as good at this as him,' Amare announced from across the boat. 'The cuttlefish are much too quick for me.'

Eventually, Bomal poked me with the handle. 'You try,' he said. I wrapped my fingers around the bamboo and bent my knees. I held the net out over the water, and readied myself with slow, deep breaths.

My first dip was premature – the cuttlefish, still a distance from the surface – comfortably diving beneath. Overcompensating on the next attempt, my prey was already half a metre out of reach when the net broke the water's surface. Third time, I missed by even further and, in my eagerness, managed to thrust the pole from my body, lose grip of the handle, and send the whole thing overboard. Bomal fixed me with a glare. I felt like I had just watched da Vinci paint the Mona Lisa then stabbed myself in the eye with the paintbrush.

Much simpler tasks would be bungled. As we reeled our first proper fish in, I was asked to break up the fifteen-litre cube of ice with a wooden stake, so that the smaller fragments of ice could refrigerate the catch in a Styrofoam box. Within a minute, I had snapped the stake clean in half. 'I've been using that to break up ice for years,' Amare muttered. We were forced to do the job with its blunt remains for the rest of the day.

Later, told to fetch a rod tied to the mast, I grappled with the knot for several minutes, before Shantha strode over and swiftly withdrew the rod from next to me. It had not been tied to the boat in the first place. Half an hour later, asked to give out our GPS reading, I proudly read out the time instead of our coordinates.

By late morning, it had become clear that our luck was poor. Despite Bomal's mastery with the net, we had caught too little bait to last us till the evening and the few fish that did bite were cheap, murk-brown grouper. Of the prized red *galmaalu*, we had only three. The men had had hauls worth more than 18,000 rupees all week but today's catch, they guessed, would not fetch even a third of that. I could not help but feel responsible, particularly after they began to avoid eye-contact with me. When, compounding the misfortune, a long line snapped off just after noon, taking a sinker, hooks, and bait with it to the seabed, even Bomal began to be cold-shouldered for bringing me aboard.

But I was not quite done. On the way back to shore: one final ignominy. Leaping down from the top of the cabin, I stepped through the lid of one of their three Styrofoam containers and damaged one of the more expensive of their fish.

When we arrived at the harbour, not a word was spoken as the fish were unloaded and we paddled ashore in the canoe. Though earlier in the day I had promised to buy the men a bottle of arrack for having me aboard, by now I felt I owed them much more. Emptying my wallet of every one of its notes, I practically flung the money at my boatmates, turned on my heel, and fled the harbour, thinking that if these were the genes I had been passed on, perhaps it really was for the best that my ancestors had left the fishing trade when they did.

I was still nursing the injuries to my pride at dusk but dragged myself out of the guesthouse to backtrack a little way along the coast to Matara. It was Friday, and Erena was coming for another weekend visit. While I juddered onwards on the coastal road, she was whizzing along on the swish Southern Expressway in relative air-conditioned luxury. Outside the window of my bus passed the Indian Ocean in one if its gentler avatars. Outside hers, paddies, rubber plantations, and a few lowland tea estates.

The Expressway, another Chinese-funded Rajapakse-era project, had cut travel time between Colombo and the south by half. My favourite stretch of it is between Galle and Matara. Here, the vegetation is a stately deep green and the jackfruit trees are perpetually laden with their huge, knobbly fruit. Enlivening this stretch, also, are peafowl, who skitter suicidally across the road. They are a species of 'least concern' according to the International Union for Conservation of Nature and are almost too abundant in the south. They irk farmers whose seeds and crops they pick at and issue aggravating, throaty mating calls in the mornings.

They are unquestionably beautiful, of course, but if you think a peacock's dance is delightful, wait till you have seen one meet its end on the front bumper of a 100-kmph vehicle. Travelling south with two friends once, we had swerved to avoid a male in full regalia, missing by inches the tips of a train that streamed gloriously from its body. The bird, having blundered now into the other lane in which a mini-bus was roaring along, was forced to attempt an evasive liftoff. This only made the impact more magnificent.

There were no death squawks. No mangling. As far as I could tell, there can't have been much blood. Just a thud and, from the dead middle of the bonnet, the most sublime eruption of feathers – greens, blues, indigoes thrown up in a high, flamboyant arc, and shimmering warm tones when sunlight glinted off the ocelli. In the aftermath, the mini-bus was glamorously festooned. Who could help but feel envious when the grille of the adjacent vehicle has been pimped with nature's most magical hues, its side mirrors embedded with vivid, waving fronds? Sure, no animal deserves to meet its end this way, but if roadkill must exist, then peacocks are its most spectacular victims.

Thankfully for the birds, Erena's bus ride had been uneventful, but our weekend together would turn out to be spectacular nonetheless. On a hired scooter over the next two days, we breezed past endless seaside sweeps, visited cadjan-shack eateries and drank at inexpensive watering holes with curiously un-Lankan names like 'Tiki Bar' and 'Johnny's Pub'. Meanwhile, roadside hawkers flogged snorkeling trips, old women in long skirts sold sundresses to other women in bikinis, and a fire-breather did a circuit of the beach restaurants, imploring his audience to pay up after each of his five-minute shows.

These were the most-active protagonists of this coastal whirl – a southern working class still working out how to squeeze a profit from the tourism explosion. Rising in smouldering grey above all this and better-heeled at exploiting the tourist dollar was a 400-room eyesore bearing the Marriott name.

It is a coastline of contrast, a place of day-long idleness and evening indulgence for foreigners and of steady industry and religious fidelity for many locals. Wisps of marijuana-smoke float through the dodgy bars in Dalawella or Mirissa; then, from the shrine inside a home or near a Bodhi tree, the scent of incense comes. Near Galle, a Japanese-funded Peace Pagoda ringed by frangipani is embedded halfway up the hill. Below it, foreigners strip off and laze on the 'jungle beach' whose trees verge close on sand.

My own adventures in the south were no less conflicting. While Erena was with me, we were treated more or less like royalty, tourism operators assuming we were on an overseas holiday from the West. Restaurant tables with the best views were made available to us, keys to the nicest guesthouse rooms were smilingly handed over, and flyers advertising beachside revelry were constantly pressed into our hands. The downside was the constant roadside nagging of trishaw drivers. Although I had come to accept being looked upon as a two-week visitor when I was with her, Erena was uniformly disdainful of the experience. 'Honestly, I've lived here four-and-a-half years,' she'd fume, '... and I still get treated just like one of the other whites.' She had a growing grip on Sinhala and worked two jobs. She felt she had earned her stripes.

Then, alas, Monday came, and she left for Colombo again. As had been the case right through the trip, this left me feeling sorry for myself. I travelled west along the coast and, that afternoon, traipsed mirthlessly around Galle's Dutch fort, which since post-war gentrification seemed more a tropical outpost of the Mediterranean than the quaint Sri Lankan village it had once been.

It was uncanny, also, that the most unsavoury incidents occurred soon after Erena had departed. One more lay in store for me on this trip.

It happened at nearby Unawatuna – one of the most well-touristed beaches in the country. I had just sat down at a restaurant table and put my toes in the sand when one of the restaurant's waiters approached me. He was slight, curly-haired, clean-shaven, and very young.

'We can't serve you here.' His voice was low and firm.

'What's that?' I asked.

'This restaurant doesn't serve locals.'

'I'm just here to eat. I'm not drinking.'

'Food, drink, smokes, whatever. You're a local. We can't serve you.'

This put me in an incredulous mood. There had been many reports of southern hotels refusing Sri Lankan guests but surely this kind of discrimination could not be extended to casual seaside eateries.

'Is the food here poisonous to Sri Lankans?' I asked. 'What is the reason for this?'

'What is the reason? The reason is we don't want to. If you left immediately, it would be better for you.'

Having eventually dined at a nearby joint – owned, as it happened, by a Brit – I tracked down the number of the restaurant's owner, Sujith, the next day. He tried a deflecting tactic first up.

'Yes, we weren't serving any food last night anyway,' he said.

'Then why were the food menus around? Others were eating.'

'Can't be.'

Eventually, he admitted that locals were not served as a matter of policy. From there the conversation grew hostile. Isn't his restaurant on a public beach, I demanded. Didn't the nation's taxes pay for its replenishment last year, when currents had eroded much of it away?

'So what if they paid for it?'

'Isn't it very unjust to ban the people who paid to help your business exist?'

'Unjust? Unjust? Unjust is when we have problems with local men getting drunk and harassing the foreigners. We have parties there. There are foreign women who dress differently. It's not like other beach restaurants. People come to drink also.'

Gallant fellow that I am, I will admit Sujith's point here may be a good one. Sri Lankan men are, in general, notorious for their chauvinism and misbehaviour. For almost any woman in the country, packed buses and trains are essentially a gauntlet of unscrupulous male hands. Many workplaces must also necessarily become the scene of endless rebuffing of male colleagues and bosses. And where Sri Lanka was in 1960 the first country to elect a female Head of Government, the flag the nation will proudly claim to have planted for womankind has more often been the screen behind which widespread oppression and objectification has been carried out. Female participation in government, for example, is still a pathetic 5.9 per cent – the lowest in South Asia despite Sri Lanka's high female literacy. If women politicians are subjected to lewd jibes in the midst of parliamentary sessions, it was too easy to imagine that tourists in beachwear would be hassled at bars late at night.

And yet, that is only a mild defence for Sujith. It was not merely groups of handsy men who he banned from his restaurant, but all Sri Lankans – women, couples, everyone. I attempted to make this point.

'If men are the problem, it would make sense just to keep out the troublemakers, wouldn't it?' I asked. 'I'm sure it's not that hard to figure out what kind of customer is going to hassle the foreigners. Isn't that better than throwing on a blanket ban?'

He seethed. 'Look here. You're coming from Colombo, pointing your finger and telling me how to run my restaurant. You don't have a clue. Why don't you come this afternoon to the restaurant? I will be there. Then we will see.'

'Is that a threat?'

'That of course is for you to decide. You can take it how you want.'

'Look, I'm just saying that you don't have to ban the entire race ...'

'Here, don't try to pull me into a race game. This is not about race or politics. This is a business. Even if Indians come, they will be treated like locals.'

'Err... what?'

'This is not a race thing. Indians are also not allowed to eat here.'

Later that day, after a little more mirthless traipsing in Galle, I collected my things, rounded the southwest curve of the island on a train, and decided, out of some misguided sense of nostalgia, that before I properly exited the south, it might be nice to spend a night at Hikkaduwa.

During the height of the war, Hikkaduwa had been one of the few destinations to which my parents once ventured on a day trip. The outing had been much anticipated. I remember the excitement between my sisters and I, the evening before our excursion. There was a pre-dawn rousing, and then a half-asleep trek to the Dehiwala bus halt. There were happy hours in the shallow water, with reef fish nibbling my feet and floaters slipping around my matchstick arms. Then, finally, flashes of the train home at dusk, a book in one hand, and a packet of spicy chickpeas on my lap.

But this was the Hikkaduwa of the 1990s. The town has since been transformed into a three-kilometre tourist trap. There are still familiar glimpses of coastal Sri Lanka if you look closely – the hawker falling asleep beside clusters of thambili, the fishmonger flogging his final basket of *salaya* in the afternoon heat. But overpowering all this was Hikkaduwa's relentless warping of itself into the tourists' ideal of a tropical seaside town. There is no dhal, or sugar, or chillies at many corner shops, instead: brightly-coloured bikinis, board shorts, and overpriced souvenirs. The restaurants may have one 'rice-and-curry' item, but most will offer menus in Russian script and feature slightly spicier variants of Continental cuisine under the 'Sri Lankan food' heading.

But then, why should this part of the island refrain from selling itself, even shamelessly? The place might have few delights for me (intrepid adventurer I felt I had become), but tourism has forged a path to riches for some and become a financial safety net for many others. Occasionally, even the learned and astute found employment in the industry.

In fact, it had been along this length of coastline where I once had one of the most stimulating discussions about the state of the nation with a man who happened to be waiting tables at a restaurant. His name was Susantha – a college graduate, which means he was among the roughly five per cent of school-leavers who achieve entry to the country's nationalized universities. That evening, he had introduced me to many well-formed theories on how post-war Sri Lanka might strengthen itself.

'It's vital that we get better technology to our growers, don't you think?' he had asked, at one point. 'We're an agricultural economy, so there are obvious benefits when it comes to productivity. But then, who knows, it might even spark some cultural change. If, thanks to technology, women can do more work on farms, then we might start to see them in a different light in the provinces. Then they might have opportunities and be able to properly engage in the economy. See how village women have started driving trishaws now?

Twenty years ago, people would have laughed. Now they have the freedom to get their work done.'

He went on apace, leading me to new understandings of law and order ('We have to diversify our police force'), education ('Our children know how to rote-learn, but can they think critically?'), nationalism ('The people who understand our nation the least are the ones who shout the loudest about it'), and corruption ('Well in that area, we are fucked'). I had wondered, perhaps rudely, why he was a waiter. Why was this intelligence not being put to more appropriate use?

'I don't speak good English,' he had explained. 'Even what I have learned, I have got by working at this restaurant.' He had applied for many positions in Colombo but had been repeatedly rejected, he said. 'I could have got a job in the government, but honestly, the pay at a good restaurant is much better. I can send my son to college in Colombo now. He won't have to go through what I did.'

That evening, still in Hikkaduwa, I met a good friend who sketched out the counterbalance to Susantha's story. Uniformly punctual, lean, and athletic, Shehan wallops me witless at squash every week and is a remorseless apologist for the Colombo cabal.

'Well, it is unfortunate for the guy,' he said, after Susantha's story had somehow entered our conversation. 'But then, that is the reality.'

'But Shehan, shouldn't Sri Lanka be trying to make better use of capable people?'

'How is he going to work in a corporate office if he doesn't know English?'

'You know Sinhala,' I replied. 'And pretty much everyone in your office would know a local language. There are so many roles that don't require him to interact with anyone overseas.'

'Why doesn't he just learn English?'

'Why should he have to?'

'Because he can't get a job otherwise.'

'Shouldn't that change?'

'You know it's not going to,' he said. After a pause: 'That is the reality.'

Shehan was a third-generation alumnus of Royal College – the nation's elite state school for boys, which splays itself out across Colombo's old-money neighbourhood of Cinnamon Gardens. There is perhaps no one on the planet who adores his alma mater more. Shehan had hoped, for instance, at his wedding – one of the nation's most powerful politicians in attendance – to exit the hall to the tune of the school song, until his fiancée had shot the idea down. Conversations with him were often filled with class ranklings. 'Disciplinary standards at Royal have definitely gone down since I was there,' he once told me. 'It's all these scholarship recipients from the outstations.'

These are not altogether uncommon opinions in the capital. In many of Colombo's prissier clubs and bars, many Royalists (as old boys of Royal College call themselves) will find their complaints matched in volume and mewling pitch by graduates of St Thomas' College, the nation's most prestigious private school. Sit a Royalist and Thomian opposite each other, set them off on a conversation about the state of the nation, and sure as the weather is warm, phrases such as 'lower calibre of people' and 'uneducated fellows' will be paraded out. Before long, a screeching rant will be brought to a close by the proclamation: 'and that is why this country will never develop!'

Where for the likes of Susantha, Sri Lanka was on a journey – one that may transport it towards prosperity and modernity – for many Colombo elites, Sri Lankans were irredeemably flawed and the nation thus doomed to flounder forever. In fact, only the efforts and intelligence of themselves and their friends even prevented the place from plunging into full-scale rot and chaos. Their only point of reference is the West, and Sri Lanka was perpetually failing on every front. Why give a non-English speaker an office job when all he knows to do is walk around with snot all over his shirt and trails of toilet paper sticking out the back of his under shorts?

These elites have walled Colombo up so formidably, I have generally found there is little point in throwing stones. Better to sycophantically make friends with the men in the towers, as I will freely admit to have done. There is always the chance of gaining marginal access to their networks. There could be perks that trickle down.

This evening, I had checked into a hovel of a room with damp foam for a mattress and enormous, hairy spiders for bathroom attendants. When Shehan offered a spare bed in the four-star hotel suite he was staying in for work, I was only too glad to accept. The next day, when I thanked him for the favour, he fixed his gaze on a distant wall, drew himself to his full height, and called up his best man-of-duty expression. 'You see,' he said. 'That is just what a Royalist does.'

Seven weeks, four train rides, hundreds of dolphins, eight islands, two safaris, four misplaced T-shirts, two pairs of wrecked flip flops, three boat rides, several elephant erection sightings, five forehead stitches, countless bus and trishaw trips, and one appallingly filthy backpack later, I had reached my final destination of the journey. I was in Sinharaja National Park – the only rainforest on the island. Even by Sri Lankan standards, the place was magnificently overrun by greenery. Vegetation swarmed every bank, scaled every hill, and waged full-scale war on every road, building, and telephone pole – on anything that was not of the forest.

Getting here had itself been something of an adventure. Tricking myself into believing I had plenty of time to make the journey, I had spent too much of the day reading at a beach near Bentota, not accounting for the infrequency of transport to what was a surprisingly remote pocket of the country. I managed to catch only the final bus of the day to Neluwa – the town that lay near the entrance to the forest. As that ride had taken much longer than I had expected, I found myself disembarking at a deserted bus stop at 9 pm and had to trouble a reluctant trishaw driver to take me onward, over the Gin river, and into the bounds of the jungle. From the forest village of Lankagama, another mode of transportation was required. A schoolteacher named Varuna – who had been alerted to my arrival by a friend of a friend of a friend – put me on his motorbike and took me up the hill to my guesthouse. Two of his colleagues escorted us on a separate motorbike so Varuna would not have to make the return trip alone. If there was one theme to my Sri Lanka travels, it was this: I kept getting into trouble through nothing but my own stupidity, and unfathomably kind strangers kept bailing me out. By this stage, this was nothing short of stupefying.

In any case, I was glad I had come to Sinharaja last because rarely have I fallen in love with a place faster. Even its inconveniences were charming. There was no electricity during the day but that is only because Lankagama – the sole inhabitation on the southern side of the park – is powered by its own mini hydro turbines, unconnected to the national grid. I had been woken too early in the morning by village chatter but that is only because folks were up tapping their coconut trees for toddy or plucking tea from garden bushes to sell to the tractor that came by once a week.

There was no cellphone coverage, no wifi, no shiny SUVs – just the warbling of a thousand birds, the babbling of a hundred brooks, and lungfuls of fresh, sweet-smelling air. All this, only 120-odd kilometres from Colombo. It might as well have been a different planet.

I was met that morning by a park officer named Jayantha. As Sinharaja is teeming with cobras, vipers, kraits, and all manner of venomous spiders, visitors must be escorted along the trails. I could not have hoped for a more knowledgeable guide. As we trekked beneath Sinharaja's dense canopy, the forest's moist detritus underfoot, I could point to just about any tree and Jayantha would reel off the Sinhala name, its possible ayurvedic usage, and, where applicable, the particular bird or animal that fed on its fruit or nested in its hollows. While I stumbled on every tree root and slipped just about on every decline – my limbs perpetually in a windmill motion as I tried to keep balance – Jayantha flitted along on 200-rupee flip flops, his arms folded behind his back as he made sure, balletic leaps over the rocks and logs obstructing the way.

I found myself intrigued by his appearance. Almost anywhere else on the planet, someone with his combination of hairstyle (shoulder-length mullet) and beard style (hairs sprouting exclusively from his neck) would be shunned from society or beaten up on a daily basis. Because he chewed betel more or less constantly, his teeth were also an iridescent techno-orange. And yet, in the wild, he was lord of this domain, spotting snakes from dozens of metres away, pointing out distant langurs in the canopy, brushing centipedes out of my path, picking up lizards to have them crawl up his arm, identifying at least two dozen birds by the sound of their call. In the village itself, which we walked through later in the day, the man was basically a rockstar – everyone seemingly overjoyed at the mere sight of him, all passers by stopping him for a chat. By evening, I felt I should perhaps ask him for an autograph.

If Jayantha had one failing, however, it was that even he could not save me from the leeches. The vegetation grows so close on the paths in Sinharaja that within the first ten minutes the trekker must make peace with the fact that he or she will be prey to a multitude of these one-inch servants of Satan.

Throughout our walks, I was constantly plucking wriggling black strips off my limbs, most times after they had already dug their anaesthetized teeth into my skin and begun the draining. One had crawled up my shirt and needed removing from the vicinity of my belly button. Another time, I felt a stirring in my shorts and – without being too graphic – had to remove a leech that needed a little … err … untangling. Almost every traveler who has visited these forests has emerged with a leech story. John Still, who spent many months in Sinharaja through the first half of the twentieth century, had come across this particularly grisly tale about a *vederala* (medicine man) who had attempted to fetch something from high in a tree.

> [The vederala] began to climb the tree, but its branches were slippery … and he fell to the earth and lay there unable to rise, for his back was injured. Then the leeches came, looping along by ones, by tens, by hundreds, and at last in such myriads that his whole body was covered by their waving multitude, and all the blood was sucked out of his veins. The men who at last found him had to light torches with which to sweep the foul tribe of blood-congested creatures [away].

Thankfully, nothing quite so grim befell me. In any case, after you have yanked the first dozen from your body, they become mere annoyance, rather than full-blown exponents of evil. Cosmic laws, such as they are, may also decree that in order to revel in Sinharaja's many delights, it is only natural a few hardships are endured. I realize I have gushed about the place enough already, but please allow me another saccharine burst.

There are waterfalls here. At least six along the trails: all of them stunning. On this day, Jayantha and myself had five of those to ourselves – the last only briefly intruded upon by a family of tourists. As if being cut off in a rainforest, amid thousands of towering trees and spectacular tropical species was not wondrous enough, you can go swimming in the pools beneath many of the falls and admire the rainforest from the water.

Twice in the day I took a dip. The first swim was at the stately Kekunu Ella – the fall just a few metres tall, but the river so broad here that rays streamed through the gap in the canopy and made rainbows amid the tumbling torrents. The second swim was at the much taller, more majestic Doovili Ella – the whole clearing shrouded in a fine spray, while the waterfall emitted a deep, resonant growl.

The next morning, I would leave the rainforest, riding out of Lankagama on a bus, taking another to Mathugama, and, from there, boarding a third that would transport me north along the coast to Dehiwala. There, the corner shop would still be buzzing with gossip, spanking new restaurants will have sprouted where old houses stood, and trucks, trishaws, and pedestrians would still be waging battle on the roads.

But before I returned to the city, I took with me one unforgettable Sinharaja memory. While Jayantha and I swam in the pool below Doovili Ella, forks of lightning began to split the sky, thunder filled the forest, and a million little plinks announced the arrival of a downpour – the water from the heavens meeting the earth's cool, clear torrents, swirling, pattering, roaring, and lifting together. It was a moment of the most breathtaking elation. Eyes closed, I wondered whether any place on the planet could be so perfect; I wondered how many times in my life I would know such bliss.

That I would reflect so highly of my time in Sinharaja is something of a surprise even to me. Because, honestly, I would never have expected to feel so positively towards a day in which I had had to evict a parasite from my nether regions.

Epilogue

Near the front, a careworn young mother sat, her two tots climbing all over her to make faces at the old man in the seat behind. Near the rear exit a middle-aged gentleman watched over the two gunny sacks of okra he had heaved aboard. At the back, a young woman was guarded by a scowling, beanie-wearing boyfriend. In the seat reserved for clergy, a child monk cracked jokes with a friend, while two foreign women fought to keep their balance, standing on the aisle beside them. I felt like I knew each one; all these characters were so familiar now. I had, with no little joy, boarded another provincial bus.

Six months had passed since I came home from Sinharaja. In that time, Sri Lanka already seemed to have changed. The coalition government had begun to come apart – its lukewarm administration not conservative enough for conservatives, not liberal enough for liberals, not effective enough for anybody. The trade unions had gained strength: Colombo forever gridlocked by some strike or protest. The cricket team … well, let's not depress ourselves. Elsewhere, negotiations had begun to lease the Hambantota port to China, families from the Vanni had carried out a months-long campaign for answers on wartime disappearances, and tourism in the south had suffered a minor dent owing to recent political instability.

Nature had not been kind either. Although the monsoon seemed to be beginning as I left the east, it had never really arrived with any meaningful strength. Drought had since taken grip in the north and east: over two million people at its mercy. There was enough to drink, for now, but crops had floundered, livestock had become gaunt, and even the wild animals had begun to die off – their ponds and waterways ravaged by the unremitting sun.

When I began my travels, I had hoped to find the nation on an inexorable forward march. Transition, however, was forever waylaid by unseen complications. Like a trishaw ride through so many little towns, there was backtracking, diversions, dead ends, potholes, hidden ditches, and people who had no interest in getting out of the way. Hope for progress remained. So did the fear that it would not come.

The bus clunked its way south out of Hatton town and into tea country. It passed workers' shabby housing, which squatted beneath immaculately kept estates. It passed sweater-clad children cycling home from school. It passed tea-plucking women trekking by the roadside, their day's take in sacks hanging from hunched backs.

The ride was enchanted by views over the tree-ringed Castlereagh and Maskeliya reservoirs but bedevilled by the hill country's steep inclines and hairpin turns. At one point, where the road was no wider than a ribbon, the engine ceased, traffic collected in all directions, and the cursing conductor set about divining the vehicle back to life. For the remainder of the journey we were never more than a few split seconds from disaster, careening from cliff-edge to precipice, as we attempted to make up for lost time.

It need not have been such a hair-raising affair but the bus did, at least, deliver us safely to Nallathanni – the village at the foot of a famous peak. Wooded and steep-sloped, the mountain beamed in the light of the afternoon sun.

No destination in Sri Lanka has captured the traveller's imaginations for as long, or as emphatically. No place is so layered in lore.

That it is the *Mahavamsa* – Lanka's Pali-language chronicle – that makes the earliest mention of the peak, and that it is this first legend which in turn inspires most of the mountain's million annual visitors, is unsurprising – such is the influence the *Mahavamsa* exerts on Sri Lankan life. According to the chronicle, it is the Buddha who left the two-metre footprint on the rock at the mountain's zenith. For about a thousand years, adherents of his religion have been drawn to the site.

Almost as ancient is Muslim veneration. The footprint, according to that tradition, belongs to mankind's progenitor Adam, who took his first earthly step on the peak following eviction from paradise. As early as 851 CE, an Arab explorer named Sulaiman makes mention of his journey to the footprint. In the following centuries, many other eminent Muslims had also come.

Hindu pilgrimage has been more recent – their belief the footprint belongs to the god Shiva probably having arisen during the reign of Rajasimha I – the Hindu king who ruled in Kandy from the last decade of the sixteenth century.

Thus did the mountain come to have at least three contemporary names. It is Sri Paadha (sacred footprint) to Buddhists, Adam's Peak to Muslims, and Sivanolipatha Malai (footprint of Shiva) to Hindus. Of illustrious mentions in historic travelogues it has also had plenty. The Chinese monk Fa-Hien mentioned the peak, as did Marco Polo, much later. Ibn Battuta had visited in person, having first seen it 'from the open sea, when we were more than nine days march distant', before summitting with the help of chains installed upon the rock. The German Daniel Pathey – a soldier in the Dutch East India Company – may have been the first European to make the climb, in 1684, but the most comically stereotypical maiden ascent, belonged, of course, to the British. A Lieutenant Malcolm had led a small expedition in 1815, and writes thus of the moment his group reached the sacred mountaintop:

> We were not, I regret to say, provided with an 'Union Jack,' but we fired three vollies, to the great astonishment of the [Buddhist pilgrims], as a memorial to them that a British armed party had reached the summit.

In the years since, Adam's Peak has had multitudes of admirers: folks who have come to worship and reflect but also to take in the peak's grandeur; to marvel at the rhododendrons; to bathe in the cool, clear headwaters from which three mighty island rivers spring; to gasp at the perfectly conical shadow the peak casts – not on the forest floor but on the carpet of clouds that lie westward in the early morning. In the valleys below the mountain, temples are tucked up against hillsides, reservoirs hug the montane contours, schoolhouses sparkle in the distance, and forests undulate in all directions; all of this, profoundly, unutterably enchanting.

I had always wanted to end my travels with this climb but the pilgrimage season only goes for half a year and my main journey had concluded in the off-season. So here I was, in late April, at the eastern foot of the peak.

It is easier to make the climb now than it had been in earlier centuries – the ancient chains having long since been replaced by concrete staircases. But that is not to say it was a cinch.

Nallathanni's elevation, I had read, was about 1,200 metres. I dragged myself out of bed and out of the guesthouse at 2 am, which gave me a little over three hours to ascend the remaining thousand if I was to see the sunrise from the top. While the trail was lit by amber lamps – a golden cord meandering up the forested slope – the mountain stood hard and black against a twinkling sky – its steepness daunting now that I was setting out to summit. In fact, I wondered if I had not left it too late, if I would make it up in time for the first rays.

And before you can even properly start on the trail, there is a maze of multicolour hodgepodge stores to navigate, many of these beneath *takaran* awnings. On sale was incense, miniature religious statues, oil for lamps, and flowers for offering, but also T-shirts, caps, dresses, sweets, reed baskets, plastic toys, and inflatables. You may have come to pay homage to the Buddha or Lord Shiva. But before any of that, commerce must have its place.

Just as I gained the main concrete path, I began to encounter groups of pilgrims – mostly dressed in white – who were making their descent. Within minutes I found myself heckled by teenagers striding down the hill. 'Ah yes, yes. Well done. Keep climbing, *aiya,*' a young man hollered as he approached, wearing a grin so smug I could sense a punchline was coming. 'You're almost at the top. Just make it around this corner and the footprint will be right there in front of you.' His companions flew into howls of laughter.

Among these groups, also, were people I could barely believe had made it all the way up. Hunched, frail, grey-haired old men and women, descending one tiny movement at a time. It must have taken them twelve hours at least to make the summit. How long had these groups spent up here? A day? Longer? Other pilgrims had infants and toddlers with them. Slightly older children – five- and six-year olds – descended on foot, their even-younger siblings asleep on parents' shoulders.

It was the foreign tourists who appeared to impress pilgrims the most. 'Look at these people who have come so far, from their country, to pray at Sri Paada,' one older woman told a companion as two young Europeans passed by. 'Huffing and puffing up the mountain at this time of night – they are also doing this because they have *bhakthi* [piety], no?'

Further ahead, about an hour's climb later, less endearing conversations were being had. A group of about twenty young men, accompanied by a young Buddhist monk, crowded a staircase. Two of their number were preaching to an older man who was resting on one of the steps. '*Aiyo*, no point talking about the head monk at the Sri Paada temple,' one of the young men told the older man. 'He's a thief. An absolute thief. Must be making millions from selling this holy place to the Muslims.'

I figured them instantly for chauvinist agitators. To confirm: I was served a pamphlet as I approached the group. It began, in Sinhala:

> Did you know we are losing our grasp on the sacred footprint? We should not just watch and let it happen. Today, the keys to Nallathanniya's vehicle compound and even the keys to the Buddhist complex, is owned by a Marrakkalaya [Muslim] policeman by the name of Farook. A Muslim has also acquired the tender to operate the bathroom facilities near the waterfall. Soon, the tender to run the shops along the path will also be acquired by them . . .

On and on the diatribe went, warning of a grand Muslim conspiracy involving Arab funds, the purchasing of nearby tea estates, the building of a grand mosque, and a secret path to the summit for use exclusively by Muslims. All this, the pamphlet warned, will transform the mountain 'into Mecca'.

A part of me wanted to tell them what I'd learned about the island's Muslims: that they had been a boon to so many Sinhala and Tamil kingdoms; that they had been vital allies of Kandyan rulers through Portuguese and Dutch persecutions; that only since 1800 had this peace been frayed. In fact, on this particular mountain, tolerance towards all religions had persisted well into the twentieth century – John Still reflecting thus in his 1930 book:

> Among the pilgrims [to the mountain] I have seen people of a half a dozen races, with as many languages, and at least four distinct religions beside many sects, and I can testify to their reverence; for the East understands religion, whereas we of the West have made of it a form of warfare.... The tolerance of the pilgrims seemed a thing that might well have been studied by Western ecclesiastics with honour and amazement, perhaps even with shame.

Tempting as it was to deliver this history lesson, these did not seem like people who put much store in facts or reason. I also did not want to be beaten up. I climbed on.

Awaiting me further up were more unwelcome sights. Strewn in the forests surrounding the walkway was all manner of trash: polythene bags rasping against tree roots, plastic bottles were glinting from the undergrowth, bits of half-eaten food left to rot beside staircases. Here is something else I had encountered on my travels: a nationwide disdain for the environment. On so many bus rides, garbage had been flung out of windows into the drains and ditches that flanked the roads and, on so many beaches, refuse had been left to the potential doom of marine life.

Especially galling was the indifference with which pilgrims littered here – at a place so many considered holy – their very act of worship accompanied by a small desecration. Close to the summit, where it is customary for first-timers to run a white thread up the length of a section where the Buddha is said to have mended his own torn robe, pilgrims scattered on the staircase the polythene packets thread had been sold in. I was reminded then of Saman and Shiromi, folks who had grown to despise the hypocrisies that had wormed their way into the practice of their religion.

But then, at the temple complex at the summit, Sri Lanka won me over again. Somehow, it always did. I arrived about forty minutes before daybreak and, having paid a visit to the footprint (which was almost totally obscured by flowers), I sat down on the concrete terraces on the eastern side of the complex. Soon, a little boy no older than seven was led to a beanie-wearing policeman a few metres away.

Policeman: [Dropping to haunches to meet the child eye-to-eye] 'You can't find your family, *putha*?'

Boy [almost in tears]: 'I can't find my *aachchi* [grandmother].'

Policeman: 'It's ok. I will help you. Do you know her name?'

Boy: 'Yes.'

Policeman: 'What is it?

Boy: 'It's *aachchi*.'

Once everyone in the vicinity had had a giggle, three young men rose and began to move from group to group to inquire if anyone had lost a child. Within minutes the boy was reunited with his aachchi. The policeman directed them up the steps and found them seats from which the sunrise would be visible, people happily making space. The boy fell asleep immediately and would miss the spectacle.

Meanwhile, I had begun to feel the wind-chill. Somehow, I had forgotten I was ascending an exposed mountaintop and had taken no warm clothes. Noticing my discomfort, a stranger sitting nearby lent me the blanket his family had spare. 'I don't think I've ever heard of anyone climbing Sri Paada by themselves,' he told me. 'Good to see something different.'

These kindnesses were neither major nor particularly consequential, but they were plentiful. They brought to mind all the good turns I had been done during the trip. I remembered Varuna and his escort in Sinharaja; I thought of the Jaffna woman who left her roadside stall to lead me half-a-kilometre to the city's museum in the blazing heat; I thought of the eastern man who, unprompted, cut me a thambili to drink when I had walked to a Batticaloa bus halt hauling bags, exhausted. Kids shared their vadai with me on trains; and I had had more invitations to home-cooked meals all around the island than I could accept.

This generosity, I felt, I had begun to reconcile with the island's many great follies. Maybe it was to endure our own idiocy that Sri Lankans held each other up. Perhaps we had no choice but to band together to survive the gits we elected to parliament, to endure the more moronic customs that have been passed down, or to withstand the dysfunction we ourselves devise.

In the coming weeks, floods and landslides would devastate western and southern pockets of the island, leaving well over 200 dead, and about 600,000 displaced. But when the comically inept government failed to respond with any semblance of speed or efficacy, citizens would put together what was hailed internationally as one of the best civilian relief efforts in the world. Thousands of volunteers would spring into action and donations of bedding, clothes, medicines, and essential sanitary goods would come in torrents. Those in unaffected parts of the island would organize a 'take my lunch' initiative, through which home-cooked food would be collected and delivered to the displaced. Where once I had passed kind deeds off as isolated moments of personal virtue, through the course of my travels I had become aware of a common wellspring of goodness. It was those with the least to spare, who often drew deepest.

Eventually, the first grey light of dawn arrived and the crowd stood to their feet and faced east. This was followed by a little commotion. Groups of tourists realized they were badly positioned to see the sunrise and shuffled themselves to the staircase in front of the terrace, obscuring the view of a whole section of locals. There was grumbling and jostling for position until a man at the back piped up: '*Aney pau* – be nice. This must be these foreigners' first sunrise. They probably don't have it where they are from.'

With that, the first rays leapt over a ridge, the lakes twinkled, the forests glowed, and as the trumpet of the kovil pooja began to fill the air, the darkness that had enclosed us dissolved into day.

Afterword

Seven stories down from my apartment balcony, a peacock that has made its way unexploded up the highway, all the way to Dehiwala, hides out by a coconut tree, as hefty raindrops make the palm fronds shiver.

The northeast monsoon arrived mercifully early. For the past two weeks, brooding skies have unleashed downpours across the island, making little ponds out of the potholes on my road, fat streams out of the runnels that come down from the hills, and rippling seas of the man-made lakes in the north-central province. Most importantly, they've filled up the reservoirs whose torrents spin the turbines that, right now, generate most of the island's electricity. The government-issue blackouts are down to roughly two hours this week.

This is late October 2022. It has not been a good year for power.

In the sticky heat of March, the blackouts ran for ten hours some days, thirteen on others, tipping the country into tumult. Sri Lanka had voted the Rajapaksas in again. In the aftermath of the 2019 Easter Attacks, carried out by Islamist terrorists, what choice did the nation have but to bring the racists back? But then, when we realized the family responsible for the resplendent waste seen in Hambantota was incapable of running a twenty-first-century economy, what choice had we but to toss them out?

'How dare these pricks abuse the power we handed to them the same way they abused it before the previous time we got sick of them?'

In July, hundreds of thousands of mostly young Sri Lankans stormed the presidential secretariat, the presidential lodgings, the prime minister's official house, and later that week, the prime minister's office. The state had stationed military and police outside each of these buildings. I was at some of these protests, breathing in the tear gas, an act that seemed a badge of civic honour at the time. You almost wanted to waft it into your airways, like a chef over a redolent broth.

Once the crowd was inside, cries went up urging restraint and respect. 'Look around, but remember everything here belongs to the public. We're the ones who will have to pay if anything is damaged.' Outside, lilting melodies of patriotic songs washed over the manicured lawns, groups of singers harmonizing over the strumming of a guitar, while the armed men who had just been overwhelmed stood around nearby.

The government attempted to label the protests merely an act of youthful merrymaking. The propaganda was not without a sprinkling of truth. A 'beach party at Galle Face', said one pro-government television host, and if you traipsed through Colombo's main protest site in its most manic months, joyful dancing and singing coexisted with furious chants, as citizens held up banners accusing the president of coming to power on a 'river of blood'. Thousands watched harrowing performance art that accused the government of hiding evidence relating to the Easter Attacks, as children blew bubbles and chased each other through the middle of the act. Emotions were turned way up. In one tent, mothers of the war-disappeared cursed the land that held them in such contempt; fifty metres away, a crowd grooved to baila, their mirth a chisel, whittling away at their pain in a year of history-making woe.

On 13 July, as protesters attempted to take the prime minister's office, some were flat on the pavement, eyes red and barely breathing after the tear gas had shocked their system. While I watched from atop the roof of a truck, a mass of tens of thousands of bodies pressing at a gate guarded by men with guns, an unconscious young man was carried out by panicked friends. Later in the day we learned that someone had died here – his lungs, previously damaged, unable to contend with the airborne chemicals. Many had travelled hundreds of kilometres to be in Colombo, drawn as if by the gravity of this immense national moment. Some left injured, others maimed.

But such is the might of Sri Lanka's political establishment that even this immense, months-long all-island straining could not fully upturn a political system that almost everyone agreed was appalling. Mahinda Rajapaksa resigned as prime minister, and President Gotabaya Rajapaksa was forced to flee the island in fear. But before they'd stepped down, the kleptocrats had installed a plutocrat to protect their interests. Sri Lanka's new president Ranil Wickremesinghe, a champion of the right to protest and the principles of democracy when such values suited his political brand, unleashed police and army upon the protests with fresh ferocity, sowing fear and puncturing the movement.

The morning after the new president had ordered a brutal attack on the Galle Face protest site in the dead of night, putting many in hospital, including journalists, I met a squadron of Air Force men at a public courtyard on a nearby road. We got to chatting. 'We've just been here, waiting for orders since 2 a.m.,' said one. 'Nothing, we've just been here since five," said another, who had not heard the previous reply. The first man shot the second a stern look. I knew from my early-morning doomscroll that an Air Force squadron had been among those that had viciously beaten both protesters and journalists.

Eventually they began to open up.

'We are struggling,' said an Air Force man. 'My son is sick and my wife needs to get him to a doctor, but there's no one to take them. The few people who have fuel are asking for five times the price.'

Said another: 'We're all from the same class. All our families are struggling. We feel the pain of the aragalaya (people's struggle) too.'

I'd come to realize that in an economic crisis of this scale, there are few non-casualties. Just as the wealthier professional classes who lobbied for the catastrophic policies that precipitated the crash had had half their wealth wiped out in the last few months as the rupee nosedived, these military men were another iteration of the perpetrator-victim nexus.

If this truly was the same group that had mercilessly thrashed on-duty journalists only hours before, they at least had an excuse – their galling lack of agency. If they did not do their masters' violent bidding, their families would be plunged into life-altering crises. As if out of guilt, they kept offering lines such as 'This is our profession, and we have to do what we are told.' It wasn't worth much, but it was something. Elites, meanwhile, had cut mutually beneficial deals with the politicians who'd brought about this calamity, for decades. They had chosen profits over democracy; looked the other way as terrible abuses of power occurred, reasoning that this was the system 'the masses' had produced for them, and so they must work from within it.

But if the power struggles of the economic crisis made one thing clear, it was that elites played a lead role in handing power to despots. Which in turn leaders used to mobilize men such as these Air Force officers, who then had become enthusiastic wielders of violence, even against those with whom they shared common frustrations. Poverty, it has been said, obliterates the future.

When I travelled into the agricultural heartlands in early and mid-August for a story about the food crisis, I realized the situation had changed plenty since I'd last been out. There was a casual disrespect for clergymen, at times monks being shouted down in buses for forcing the elderly out of their seats. This was in the north-central province, in the regions around Dambulla, Polonnaruwa, and Anuradhapura – a part of the country that was deeply Buddhist and brain-deadeningly conservative. The economic crisis had doubtless changed Sri Lankan livelihoods, but it had also changed Sri Lankan life, at least in the southern parts of the country. The clergy (not just Buddhist) that had ushered the Rajapaksas in had begun to feel the ire of a distressed electorate.

Although the protest movement had been crushed by the new president, the ideas it had brought forth had taken root. Young Sri Lankans were less wedded to the idea of a Sinhalese–Buddhist state than their parents, more awake to the world. The anti-establishment parties had gained a following. But the fresh converts came warily. Politicians were public servants who should be prevailed upon to do the people's bidding. Who paid their salaries? Who should they be accountable to? What had the political elite done in more than seventy years of post-Independence history? This was a political consciousness that had radiated across hundreds of kilometres from the tents and loudspeakers at the 'beach party' in Colombo.

There was much that remained unchanged, of course. Polonnaruwa's dogs still hated me, this powerful enmity passed down the generations so even puppies were yapping at me as I walked to a guesthouse during the course of this reporting trip. Colombo's upper crust was no less pretentious, though Kandy still looked down its nose at the capital, and Galle still pitched itself as the lovable getaway.

In Hambantota, the grand monuments the Rajapaksas built to their own outsize egos – the airport, a convention centre, the secretariat, the port, the cricket ground – continued to languish, now concrete testaments to the waste that had ruined a nation.

But there was hope still, in the mirth, in the way that Sri Lanka had begun thinking of a newer, better version of itself. And I think still of my tumble in a trishaw in Kandy, and of the kind stranger that got me through that night.

Acknowledgements

The first essay I ever wrote, way back in Grade 2, was on one of our very rare family trips to the hill country. My mother sat with me for hours and introduced me to basic sentence structure, elegant variation and the meaning of the word 'picturesque'. Thank you, Amma. And thank you, Thaththa, for teaching me how to strive. Sylvana and Manelka – your encouragement has been such a source of strength.

To friends and family who read chapters or chunks – Damith Sabah, Tom, Sid V, Mel, Ben, Elijah, Ahilan, Ceri and especially Niren, who read the whole thing – my deepest thanks. Shehan, who tolerated my pathetic sob sessions when I thought it was going badly – I'm grateful for that too.

To Shruti, who urged me to give the book a brain, and a heart – I appreciate your interventions immensely.

Erena, I don't really know how to put my profound gratitude to you on paper. How can I thank you for one specific thing, when there is such a multitude of things? Beyond everything you did to make this book happen (you moved mountains), you see me at my lowest and still choose to fill my life with joy. Thank you.